The Emergence of the Indian Best-Seller

Chetan Bhagat and His Metro Fiction

Reena Sablok

PUBLISHERS & DISTRIBUTORS (P) LTD

Published by

PUBLISHERS & DISTRIBUTORS (P) LTD
7/22, Ansari Road, Darya Ganj,
New Delhi-110002
Phones : +91-11-40775252, 23273880, 23275880, 23280451
Fax : +91-11-23285873
Web : www.atlanticbooks.com
E-mail : orders@atlanticbooks.com

Branch Office
5, Nallathambi Street, Wallajah Road,
Chennai-600002
Phones : +91-44-64611085, 32413319
E-mail : chennai@atlanticbooks.com

ISBN: 978-81-269-1853-9

Printed in India at Nice Printing Press, A-33/3A, Site-IV,
Industrial Area, Sahibabad, Ghaziabad, U.P.

Dedicated to

My husband

Ram Prakash Kapoor

Special thanks to
Dr K.K. Kapoor
(Retd. Prof. Bareilly College, Bareilly)

Preface

The present work is the outcome of my studies in the modern and contemporary Indian English Literature. It aims at showing the distinctive achievement of Chetan Bhagat as a novelist with special reference to his exploration of the best-seller phenomenon. The significance of Bhagat lies in the fact that he has dealt with the social, political, religious and racial conditions of the Indian milieu in an allegorical manner. It would be no exaggeration to say that Bhagat is the incomparable Indian English novelist of our age.

No work of this kind can possibly be completed without the assistance of eminent persons and institutions. In this connection, I may express my indebtedness and thanks to the K.M.V.P.G. College Library, Bareilly, The National Library, Calcutta, The Bombay University Library, and especially the Sahitya Akademi Library, New Delhi, for providing me with a number of books and journals. I also wish to acknowledge my indebtedness to my self-sacrificing family that so very kindly winked at my negligence of household responsibilities in my pursuit of academic excellence. Over and above all is my gratitude to my guide and mentor, Dr. K.K. Kapoor, Reader and Head (Retd.), Department of English, Bareilly College, Bareilly, who inspired me to fight on against heavy odds. Without his help and encouragement, this project could never have come to a successful end.

Reena Sablok

Introduction

Ah, Love! could I and thou with Fate conspire
To grasp this sorry Scheme of Things entire!
Would not we shatter it to bats—and then
Re-mould it nearer to the Heart's Desire!

One remembers this famous Rubai of Omar Khayyam as one reads any functional work of Chetan Bhagat,—an author who has echoed the sentiments of young India in his immensely popular novels and columns. His best-sellers are hugely entertaining, but at the same time headed with serious purpose. He has bridged the gulf between the best-seller and high brow. His novels are highly entertaining and, at the same time very slick, real, sophisticated and mainly based on metropolitan common man. His publication figure has literally reached over a million copies for each work and remains a milestone for Indian English Novel. He closely resembles Vikram Seth in his iconoclastic irreverence for the holy cows of traditional India. His characters are not ready to offer simple conformism. They are social rebels who remind us of the Angry Young Men that dominated English fiction in the 1950s. His novels are not set in the laid-back milieu of small-town India; they are right in the hustle and bustle of metropolitan Indian cities where life moves at a fast pace and change is preferred to continuity.

Chetan Bhagat's first book *Five Point Someone—What not to Do at IIT* (May 2004) is a novel about three boys who join IIT Delhi and try to cope with the notoriously heavy workload of the institute. This book has continued to stay on the India Today Bestseller List ever since its publication (190 weeks in January, 2008). It won him the Society Young Achiever's Award in 2004 and the Publisher's Recognition Award in

2005. The novel is set in the Indian Institute of Technology, Delhi, in the period 1991 to 1995. It is about the adventures of three mechanical engineering students—Hari Kumar (the protagonist), Ryan Oberoi and Alok Gupta, who fail to cope with the grading system of the IITs and come to be known as Five Pointers due to their "perennially low 5 points something GPAs". Most of the book deals with the numerous attempts by the trio to cope with and/or beat the system as well as Hari's fling with Neha who just happens to be the daughter of Prof. Cherian, the domineering head of the Mechanical Engineering Department. The tone of the novel is humorous, though it takes some dark turns every now and then, especially when it comes to the families of the main characters. Most of the action, however takes place inside the campus as the boys, led by the ever creative Ryan, frequently lament how the internationally lauded IIT system has stifled their creativity by forcing them to value grades more than anything else.

One Night @ the Call Center or *ON@CC* is Chetan Bhagat's second novel, first published in 2005. The novel revolves around a group of six call center employees working in Connexions Call Center in the Delhi suburb of Gurgaon, Haryana. It is filled with a lot of drama with unpleasant things happening to all of the leading characters. The story takes a dramatic and decisive turn when they get a phone call from God. The story begins with a train journey from Kanpur to Delhi. During the journey, the author meets a very beautiful girl. The girl offers to tell the author a story on the condition that he has to make it his second book. After a lot of hesitation the author agrees. Claimed to be based on a true story, the author chooses a person named Shyam Mehra (alias Sam Mercy) as the protagonist who is one among the six call centre employees featured. He lives in Gurgaon, Haryana with his parents. He is portrayed as an average Joe, someone who can be easily related with his ex-girlfriend Priyanka working in the same call centre as he does. He loves her even after breaking up and is quite frequently shown dreaming about the good and bad times that he spent with her. One of the reasons for his break up was that Priyanka's mother didn't approve of Shyam as team leader. Shyam tries his best to be a team leader, but his current manager Bakshi, disapproves of him on the contention that Shyam is not a go-getter. Shyam works with Vroom on a Troubleshooting Website, a project that he hopes would showcase his abilities as a team leader. He is confused as he doesn't know who he hates more—his boss, Bakshi or Priyanka's mother. However after getting a phone call from God, he gains his confidence, takes his revenge on Bakshi and wins over the love of his life, Priyanka. One of the silent features of this novel is that all the characters featuring in this novel have a dramatic and disturbing event during the night when they receive a call from God. Shyam is very upset to learn that Priyanka is engaged to a person called Ganesh Gupta who works at Microsoft in the U.S. To add to his woes, he is horrified to learn that Bakshi had cheated him, and Vroom by submitting the Troubleshooting Website to the Boston centre as his own without crediting himself and Vroom. Priynka is first happy when she is engagaged to Ganesh Gupta, who works for Microsoft, but becomes furious when she hears that her parents have planned her marriage the very next month, which she feels is too early. Both her mother and Ganesh press her to agree to her proposal. She is even more saddened by the fact that Shyam was eavesdropping on her conversation with Ganesh. When Vroom and Shyam show her that Ganesh had forged his pictures to hide his baldness, she disapproves Ganesh for having cheated her. Esha had earlier done a compromise by sleeping with a designer to get a modelling contract. However, the guy turned out to be opportunistic as he betrays her by saying that she can't become a model due to her height. He also tries to console her by sending her some money. Esha feels terribly betrayed and tries to suppress the mental pain by inflicting herself with the physical pain by purposely cutting her skin. Vroom is shocked to learn that Bakshi has cheated him and Shyam by submitting their work as his own. To add to his miseries, he overhears Esha telling the other girl that she had slept with a designer to get a modelling contract. Radhika, who loved her husband very much, is shocked to learn about his dark side of showbiz. When Vroom calls up her husband portraying as a radio-jockey and asks him to dedicate roses and a song to someone special, he chooses his girlfriend Payal, over his wife. Radhika who listens to this gets terribly upset as her husband betrays her. Military uncle tries to be nice to his son and grandson. But when he sends some pictures via mail to his grandson, his son loses his cool and asks him to keep out of his life. This leaves military uncle heartbroken.

The phone call from God is one of the salient features in the novel. The author has represented God as a friendly figure rather than a boss. He is shown as speaking in modern English rather than the stereotypical pure English or Latin that one usually encounters God speaking. The circumstances in which the characters of the novel get a phone call from God are discussed in the book. In order to cheer themselves up, all the lead characters of the novel decide to go and enjoy at a night club. After enjoying for a while, they leave for office. Midway through the journey, Vroom starts to feel nauseated after drinking alcohol and so they stop and venture out. Vroom throws up and also breaks the window pane of a shop, thus spreading an alarm. They rush out of the place in fear. While returning, they face a life-threatening situation when their Qualis crashes into a construction site and is hanging over a mesh of iron construction rods. As the rods begin to yield slowly they start to panic. They are unable to call for help as there is no mobile phone network at that place. In this situation, Shyam's mobile phone starts ringing. This is a call from God. God speaks to all, one by one and gives them suggestions to improve their life. After that, God also advises them on how to get their vehicle out of the construction site. This conversation with God motivates the group to such an extent that they all plan together to teach their boss a lesson, to improve the call centre's business and go after what they wanted.

The Three Mistakes of My Life is the third novel written by Chetan Bhagat. The book was published in May 2008 and had an initial print-run of 200000. The novel follows the story of three friends and is based in the city of Ahmedabad in Western India. It is set in the year 2000, when a young boy in

Ahmedabad, called Govind dreams of starting a business and is based on real events. To accommodate his friends Ishaan and Omi's passion, they open a cricket shop. However, each has a different motive: Govind's goal is that he just wants to be with his friends. During the story the characters have to deal with religious politics, earthquakes, riots, unacceptable love and their own mistakes. The central consciousness in the novel, Govind is an ordinary guy with which anybody can relate. He has very few desires but is obsessed with the desires he covets. His main ambition is to become a businessman. His best friends are Omi and Ish. He also loves Vidhya. Govind does not quite believe in God and is an agnostic. Friendship, Business and Mathematics are the most important things of his life. He is the narrator of the story. Ishaan is a big cricket freak and also patriotic at heart. Ishaan has been the best cricketer in his locality and school. He helps Govind by organising daily cricket coaching camps. He has a family which makes life worse for him. His father constantly nags him and his mother worsens the situation by keeping quit. He has a younger sister, Vidhya about whom he is quite protective. Omi is the son of the Hindu priest of the local temple. His family enjoys great respect among people. He is a bit dumb kind of boy and has not many dreams, but likes to concentrate on having a healthy body. However, he resents growing up and being a saint like his father. He is a religious person and actively takes part in his maternal uncle's (Bittoo Mama) religious politics. He is however confused about his religious views which are mainly influenced by Bittoo Mama. Vidya is Ishaan's sister. She is a rebel at heart and dreams to break free from the constraints of a typical middle-class society, to go to Mumbai and do a course in PR and be independent. She however despises Maths which is required for her medical entrance exams. Hence, Ish asks Govind to take Maths tuition. However, during their tuition sessions they fall in love; have intimate sexual relations, which is unacceptable by anyone. Only Omi figures out the relationship Govind and Vidya share and also reminds about the consequences of Ish getting to know about it. Ali is a student in Ish's coaching classes and a great cricketer because of nature's rare gift. However, he doesn't play too much cricket as he gets tired soon and enjoys playing with marbles. He is Muslim boy and respects Ish like a guru. He too, like Ish is patriotic at heart. He denies the offer of an Australian scholarship and wants to play in the Indian side. Bittoo Mama is the maternal uncle of Omi and belongs to a Hindu political party. He follows the preachings of Parekj-ji, a political-cum-spiritual leader and has complete faith in him. He has his horns locked with Ali's father who belongs to a secular party. He has a son, Dhiraj and he is not fond of Govind as he is an agnostic. He is the main antagonist of the story. *The Three Mistakes of My Life* highlights the dangerous mix of religion, politics, and economics that is the hallmark of contemporary India.

Chetan Bhagat's fiction touches an emotional chord in the new emerging Metro generation in India. His Metro Fiction shows the dreams and hopes of an aggressively ambitious generation whose laughter is tinged with tears. His characters are irreverent young people whose motto in life is—Get Going or Get out of the Way.

Yet there remains a pall of gloom about these bright young people, an existential angst about their future and an unrelenting presence of their past. This curious blend of humour and pathos, of hopes and fears, of success and failure marks his best-selling dark comedies of contemporary India.

The present critical work is an outstanding story of Chetan Bhagat's achievement as a novelist and socio-political activist. It is a pioneering effort as it treats across a new territory. I am sure that the readers will find the serious purpose that lies behind the apparently flippant mode that Chetan Bhagat likes to adopt. This work shall give the rising star of Indian English Fiction the academic distinction he richly deserves.

Reena Sablok

Contents

The Making of a Best-Seller

The Indian English novel as it emerged around 1930's had some well-defined features. The works of R.K. Narayan, Raja Rao and Mulk Raj Anand, though vastly different, had some basic similarities. Their fiction focused on small-town middle class folk of India's backwaters. The central theme remained 'East-West Encounter' and its effect on the Indian tradition. The preferred narrative mode for these pioneers was mythic, and their target audience a handful of English-educated middle class people.

It was Q.D. Leavis who categorized fiction according to its target audience. In her epoch-making critical treatise, *Fiction and the Reading Public,* she labeled certain novels as high-brow, fiction that everyone praised and nobody read unless it was prescribed as a textbook. Then there was low-brow fiction that everyone enjoyed reading but nobody wrote critical commentaries about.

Q.D. Leavis asserted that her evaluation of English fiction was a study in Social Anthropology. Time and again she uses the image of an iceberg in her analysis of English fiction. Her idea is that literature is an integral part of a country's culture. In a later essay 'A Glance Backward, 1965' she explains how the iceberg metaphor relates to her study of literature, specially in *Fiction and the Reading Public.* She writes:

> I wanted to find out what part the reading-public has played in determining the form and quality of English imaginative writing. For my purpose Literature (with a capital L) was simply the part of the iceberg that

> showed above the water, though this top section, and not the whole, was what was then selected as proper to be studied by university students. In fact, when my book appeared in 1932, a leading senior academic of the Cambridge English School, writing an article on 'English Studies at Cambridge,' held it and me up to opprobrium, since, he said, to read best-sellers (as popular fiction was then contemptuously labelled) showed a depraved taste and was quite outside the literary field. I felt that part—the major part—of the iceberg had been submerged by the passage of time but was still not negligible from my point of view, since having been read with pleasure by so many it must tell us something Important about the formation and taste of the reading-public at any given time, and the climate of Literature is determined by public taste to a great extent.[1]

Q.D. Leavis wants to emphasize that serious fiction Literature (with a capital L) is in no way superior to popular fiction. The serious novels form only the tip of the iceberg that is visible; the vast body of the iceberg that is under water and invisible forms the base of popular literature that must be duly recognized. She asserts that popular fiction:

> is not negligible because, first, it has been read with pleasure by many readers and, second, gives us insight into the formation and taste of the reading public at any given time. She then adds, though perhaps by this point the sentence has run on, and the climate of literature is determined by public taste to a great extent. The additional thought is, however, necessary to her overall argument as she endeavors to show in Fiction and the Reading Public that the climate of literature at any time is shaped by diverse elements of public taste. This is what she always argues following her anthropological approach to literature.[2]

Apparently, Q.D. Leavis wanted to give popular literature a thorough critical appraisal. She disagreed with the view that elite fiction is good art while popular fiction is not worth a second look. Actually this disjunction between good and popular fiction happens to be a typical 20th century phenomenon. Jane Austen, Walter Scott, Charles Dickens and Thomas Hardy were good as well as popular. Arnold Kettle's comment on this schism in 20th century English fiction is worth quoting. He writes:

> The most striking and in some respects the most alarming feature in the development of the novel in the twentieth century has been the ever-increasing separation between the good and the popular. On the one hand the majority of the novels most highly praised and valued by the intellectual arbiters are almost entirely unread by the mass of the people (this was not so in the days of Scott or Dickens); on the other hand, both the middle-brow best-seller and the mass-produced reading material of the majority of the people is despised and almost unread by the intellectuals. The consequences of this situation, like its causes, are numerous. Not merely has the commercialisation of literature had a disastrous effect on the general reading standards of the public, but the 'good' writer has come to be a more and more lonely and isolated figure, exploring a very limited range of experience for the benefit of a small audience of similarly placed admirers. Among the results is that good literature is (not unfairly) associated in the minds of millions with obscurity, affectation and all the intellectual and social snobbery of high-browism, while popularity has ceased to be an issue with the majority of serious writers and is even regarded with suspicion and contempt.
>
> Thus relieved from the obligation of writing literature which is in any sense of the word popular, the tendency of writers born into or acquiring the habits of the middle-class intelligentsia has been to explore with an even more obsessive intensity small specialised areas of their peculiar and generally quite atypical, sensibility. The theories of both Freudian and Jungian

> psychology have further encouraged this tendency, as have certain aspects of the writings of Dostoievsky and Proust and the remarkable and perverse achievement of Kafka. The sense of isolation of the artist intellectual in contemporary society reaches its climax in Kafka's work in which nightmare becomes reality and the individual is trapped in a world, not merely hostile to him personally, but apparently impervious to human action.[3]

Alienation, angst and pessimism became the central themes of Modern English Novel ranging from Virginia Woolf and James Joyce to Aldous Huxley and George Orwell. Still, the stream of popular fiction continued to flourish in spite of critical negligence. The best-seller became a niche word in literary hierarchy for those works that won popularity. There was no uniformity in the best-sellers; such works range from comedy and romance to detective or spy novels. But they appealed to a vast audience. P.H. Furbank comments:

> The best-seller (and here we shall only be dealing with best-selling fiction) forms a large but very recognizable category somewhere between literature proper, in the sense in which the word has been used elsewhere in these volumes and mere pulp fiction. Uncle Tom's Cabin is a best-seller in our sense, perhaps the most celebrated there has been. It is also a steady-seller.[4]

The best-seller, according to S.H. Steinberg, has dubious value as it is

> a book which, immediately on, or shortly after, its first publication, far outruns the demand of what at the time are considered good or even large sales; which thereafter sometimes lapses into obscurity, making people wonder why it ever came to the front; but which sometimes graduates into the rank of steady-sellers.[5]

P.H. Furbank, however, shows an understanding vision:

> The strongest objection to the mass organization and dissemination of culture is that it may foist off on the

> public something that it would never have positively wanted. Its menace is the menace of the trivial, the thing which is too dead and empty to have intrinsic interest, but yet is thrust down people's throats until they become accustomed to triviality and expect it. This cannot fairly be said of the best-seller, and even less of the steady-seller, for they have a life of their own and express strong needs and deeply felt beliefs.6

Furbank goes out further in the essay to analyse the intrinsic qualities of a best-seller. Any literary work cannot be created or maketed like a consumer product, through branding, packing or publicity. It has to have something extra that draws the readers to buy and read. What is that intrinsic quality?

According to Furbank,

> to have true best-seller appeal a writer must believe passionately and absolutely in what he writes. But, of course, there may very well be absolute conviction on one level and calculation at another. In her indispensible *Fiction and the Reading Public,* Q. D. Leavis quotes a number of popular authors who discuss their own artistic intentions.[7]

The point he makes is that any author who wants people to read him must have something substantial to say even though the message is sugar-coated in humour, satire or romantic fables.

Secondly, the popular author must set his eyes on a target audience that may be receptive to his ideas. He must keep his mind focused on the hopes and fears of his target group. Once the author and his target audience are tuned into a mutually responding relationship, the works are bound to win popular acclaim. Again, a best seller has powerful emotional force and, unlike high-brow fiction, it does tell a story. Another feature of the best-seller is what may be called romantic disproportion, the use of incongruity to introduce the emotion of the wonderful or the laughable. Often such incongruity is loaded with irony as philosophers become fools and fools, philosophers.

The generation of English novelists that bridged the divide between high-brow and popular literature was that of the angry young men of the 1950's. This generation created classics like John Osborne's play, *Look Back in Anger* (1956), John Wain's *Hurry on Down* (1954), Kingsley Amis' *Lucky Jim* (1955) and John Braine's *Room at the Top* (1957). These authors gave voice to the anger and frustration of the Post-war British youth that saw the decline of the Empire, and the rampant social injustice ridden with hypocrisy that dominated the British establishment. All these works signify an attitude of mind that borders on anger, though Kenneth Allsop in his famous critique, *The Angry Decode,* suggests that anger is a misnomer. He writes:

> I think the more accurate worked for this new spirit that has surged in during the fifties is dissentience. They are all, in differing degrees and for different reasons, dissentients. I use the word in preference to dissenter that implies an organised block separation from the Establishment, whereas dissentience has more modulated meaning—more to disagree with majority sentiments and opinions.[8]

The phenomeon of anger or dissentience, spread like wild fire in the middle decades of the twentieth century. Be it theatre, fiction, poetry or cinema the angry young man strutted with supreme confidence, cocking a snook at the Establishment, attacking the holy cows of totems or taboos with gay abandon. John Osborne's Jimmy Porter screamed loudly against the social hierarchy in England, recollecting his emotions not in tranquility like Sissy Wordsworth but in fire and blood. John Wain's Charles Lumley also played out a roller coaster ride across the social strata before finding his own niche in society. Kingsley Amis' Jim Dixon let loose all hell on a quiet academic institution before subduing all his perceived enemies. John Braine's Joe Lampton used all his physical attributes to attract a rich heiress and thus leap-frog over the social divide that denied him a dignified existence. In any case, these works incorporating the angry young man wiped out the artificial dividing line between high-brow and popular literature winning both critical acclaim as well as huge public demand. They opened up new possibilities for the growth of novel, and made contemporary respectable. V.S. Pritchett acknowledges this much in his preface to his landmark work, *The Living Novel*:

> The forms of the novel are various, but it has emormously developed the field of the curiosity; new country has been subjugated in every generation; and the masters are those who have first invaded and liberated and added new territory. Let us admit that changes in style, method and belief often stand between us and the immediate enjoyment of many of the great are not only because of their inherent qualities, but because they were the writers who were most sensitive to the situation of their time. They are, in the finer sense, contemporary. I do not mean necessarily that they explicitly responded to external events, though they often did; evidently even bad writers reflect the age in which they live; I mean that the great are sensitive to an intrinsic situation. We say today that we are living in an age of transition, between two worlds; the lesson of the master is that human life is always in transition; an essential part of his excellence is that he brings this clearly out in his work. We have only to glance at the second-rate novelists to see how they differ in this sense from the masters. The second-rate are rarely of their time. They are not on the tip of the wave. They are born out of date and out of touch and are rooted not in life but in literary convention.[9]

The Indian English novelists who broke away from convention to write best-sellers depicting reality with dollops of black humour and irony are Salman Rushdie and Vikram Seth. Salman Rushdie's *Midnight's Children* has emerged as a classic in its depiction of India's partition in 1947 as a social, political and psychological disaster for the succeeding generations. Another significant contemporary best-seller that analyses Indian's Post-Colonial reality is Vikram Seth's *A*

Suitable Boy (1993). The fable of this novel illustrates the black comedy genre in all its aspects. A Suitable Boy functions as a political fable, a roman a clef, showing the emerging polity of Post-Colonial India. Seth has used a variety of characters to show how in the very first decade after independence the mood of the people changed from euphoria to despondence. While debating the role of students in politics, Seth briefly mentions his central theme thus:

> Their post-independence romanticism and post-independence disillusionment formed a volatile mixture.[10]

His diagnosis is that vote-bank politics and communalism as an election tool have corroded the soul of the fledgling Indian democracy. The political characters Vikrarn Seth uses fall into three categories. In the first group there are certain national figures like Jawaharlal Nehru, Rafi Ahmed Kidwai, and Rajrishi Purushottam Das Tandon who appear in their real names. Vikram Seth minutely observes their role in Indian politics, and points out their feet of clay. In the second category are some leaders who appear with changed names but their personalities are identifiable. There is the Purva Pradesh (Uttar Pradesh) Chief Minister called S.S. Sharma who looks like a spitting image of G.B. Pant. Then there are two state ministers—the secular Mahesh Kapoor who seems to be a dramatized version of Damodar Swaroop Seth, and L.N. Agarwal who echoes the personality of C.B. Gupta. In the last group are fictional characters who represent the emergent forces in the Indian polity. Among these the two important figures are the successful subaltern, Waris Khan, and the doomed idealist, Abdur Rasheed.

Mahesh Kapoor, a freedom fighter and an idealist, stands at the core of the political fable in *A Suitable Boy*. He is a fictionalised version of Damodar Swaroop Seth, a Nehruvian from Rohilkhand whose memory is preserved in Bareilly at a park consecrated to his name. He is, in essence, a symbolic figure representing those idealistic Congressmen who were hugely disillusioned by the decadence of the Post-Independence politics. The tragic denouement of his political career is the culmination of a rapidly rotting culture when manipulation, nepotism, and communalism totally perverted the Indian political value system. As Mahesh Kapoor ultimately resigns from the Congress and joins the KMPP, he reminiscises about the genesis of the Congress infighting, and the resultant dilution of political ethics. Since Independence the Congress had been split between the leftist followers of Nehru, and the conservative right-wing led by Sardar Patel. The Patel loyalists saw:

> Nehru as rootless deracinated Indian whose sentimental creed was a pro-Muslim secularism and who was divorced from the majority of his Hindu citizenry (*A Suitable Boy*, 955).

The challenge to Nehru's supremacy arose in the form of Purushottam Das Tandon who fought for, and won, the office of the Congress President in spite of Nehru's strong opposition. The inevitable Nehru-Tandon clash was set into motion by the constitution of the new Congress Working Committee. Tandon packed the CWC with his conservative colleagues, and 'did not include—and had indeed refused to indude—either his defeated opponent—Kripalani—or Kidwai, who had planned Kidwai's campaign' (p.954). The Nehruites and the Tandonites differed on ideological grounds, but most of all on the Muslim question. Nehru emerged as an astute political strategist. Outmanouvered by the Tandonite party-bosses, he played his trump card. He resigned from the membership of the CWC. Nehru's move caught the Tandon faction by surprise. They lost confidence, fearing a rout in the forthcoming General Elections. To save face, Tandon offered his own resignation from the Congress Presidency. Nehru caught the main chance and mounted a fresh offensive. Vikram Seth admires Nehru's charismatic leadership, but he is not blind to the fact that even great men like Nehru have feet of clay, and that wrong means cannot be justified on ground of noble ends. Nehru regains the reins of power, but he does so at the cost of alienating a huge body of Hindu Nationalists, and thus sows the seeds of a communalised polity. Vikram Seth supports the common perception that Nehru stood like a huge banyan tree under which nothing could grow.

Let us cast a glance at the political fortunes of those whom Nehru's political somersaults left in the lurch. J.B. Kripalani never regained his political eminence; Rafi Ahmed Kidwai survived as he played a double game; and Mahesh Kapoor was ruined. In the novel, Mahesh Kapoor goes back to the Nehru led Congress, but his electoral prospects are hugely damaged by his days in political exile. He is defeated by a rank outsider, Waris Khan, by dubious means, and is broken by his ignominous defeat.

Mahesh Kapoor's benefactor, the Purva Pradesh Chief Minister S.S. Sharma, is another interesting political persona in *A Suitable Boy*. He is shown as a fictionalised version of the former U.P. Chief Minister, Pt. Govind Ballabh Pant:

> Sharmaji was a rather hulking man with a perceptible limp and an unconscious and slight vibration of the head, which was exacerbated when, as now, he had a long day. He ran the state with a mixture of guile, charisma, and benevolence. Delhi was far away and rarely interested in his legislative and administrative fief. *(A Suitable Boy, 17)*

He is a good administrator; honest and impartial, with impeccable secular credentials. Yet after the General Elections he is kicked upstairs and called to Delhi. His successor, though he seems to be grooming Mahesh Kapoor for the job, is L.N. Agarwal, a rank political opportunist who plays the Hindu-Muslim card for political gains. Yet this entire clamour amounts to nothing in the world of realpolitik, and L.N. Agarwal, at the end of the novel, is all set to occupy the Chief Minister's chair in Purva Pradesh.

In the political success of people like L.N. Agarwal lies the significance of A Suitable Boy as a Post-Colonial fable. Seth finds the emergent Indian polity sliding towards two black holes—communalism and lumpenization. The shadow of communal politics looms large in this novel, objectified as a mosque-temple dispute. The Alamgiri Mosque standing cheek by jowl near an ancient Shiva Temple, is a fictional rendering of the Kashi Visvanatn-Gyanvapi Mosque dispute in Varanasi, with echoes of the Babri Masjid cacophony in the background. Seth introduces his readers to the incendiary situation in Brahmpur. As the resurgent Hindus try to rebuild the temple to consecrate the holy linga once again, Brahmpur goes up in flames. A huge riot engulfs the city fuelled by rumours and aggravated by the mismanagement of the security forces. The villain of the piece is the controversial Home Minister, L.N. Agarwal. Events reach the flash-point as that year, unfortunately, Dussehara and Moharram coincide in the lunar calendar. The Bharat Milap procession intersects the route of a Tazia procession, and all hell breaks loose. The actor playing Rama is injured in the altercation, and the crowd goes berserk. The denouement of the temple-mosque controversy in A Suitable Boy is typical of Vikram Seth's flippant irreverence and irony. The huge linga is hauled out of the Ganga bed, and dragged up the stairs of a ghat by a cartful of labourers, but it rolls back to lie in the river bed.

The threat of lumpenization of the Indian polity is objectified in the meteoric rise of Waris Khan in electoral politics. Waris is a village bumpkin, uneducated and uncultured. The Nawab of Baitar puts him up as a dummy candidate in his area during the Assembly elections to cover up the possibility of Mahesh Kapoor being denied the Congress ticket. As the elections draw near, Mahesh Kapoor's son is involved in a violent act, injuring the Nawab's son. Waris deems him now an enemy of his Nawab, and decides to defeat Mahesh Kapoor by hook or by crook. He refuses to withdraw in his favour. Finally, he manages to beat Mahesh Kapoor by the proverbial whisker. As Waris Khan, the newly-crowned MLA, visits the Baitar Fort, his erstwhile boss—the Munshi—prostrates himself at his feet, begging pardon for a thousand obscenities and indignities he may have hurled on Waris in his days of servitude. Waris is generous: "All right, you sister-fucker, I bless you" (p.1281). As Mahesh Kapoor reads his character, Waris is not as much a rogue as a fool. He would make a perfect servant, but a horrid master. He is not evil per se, but is ignorant of all that is good and noble in human character, social values and political culture.

Vikram Seth's worry is that if people like Waris are going to hold the reins of power in Post-Colonial India, she will hardly need any enemies to ruin her. It is no use blaming an individual, broods Vikram Seth, the fault lies within the system that India has chosen to govern her people. A huge crop of Waris Khan has erupted all over India, snuffing out the promising idealistic youngsters like Abdur Rasheed. Rasheed, the only truly tragic character in the novel, is a secular and educated Muslim boy who fights for the rights of the landless labourers in a feudal society. He is hounded by his people, rejected by his family, and driven to suicide. His death-scene evokes true pathos, and a tragic sense of waste. The brief scene differs from the generally mocking tone of the novel:

> Rasheed walked along the parapet of the Barsat Mahal, his thoughts blurred with hunger and confusion...
>
> No Satan, no God, no Iblis, No Gabriel.
>
> Endless, endless, endless, the waters of the Ganga.
>
> And the stars above, below .
>
> .. . and some were seized by the cry, and some we made the earth to swallow, and some we Drowned ....
>
> Peace. No. Prayers. No more prayers.
>
> To sleep is better than to pray ....
>
> A spring in paradise.
>
> O God, O God. (*A Suitable Boy*, 1315)

The triumph of Waris and the suicide of Abdur Rasheed are objective correlatives that point to the dead-ends of the Post-Colonial politics as it grew in the 1950's. Most contemporary Indian English poets and novelists are deeply aware of the Post-Colonial angst that has led to such explosions as the Sampurna Kranti led by J.P. Narayan and the recent Anna Hazare wave against corruption. However, other Indian novelists stayed away from such themes until the emergence of Chetan Bhagat in 2004.

By a delicious coincidence, Chetan Bhagat (b. 1974) is himself an angry young man deeply alive to the important issues that dominate contemporary Indian society and polity. In Indian English Novel, the barrier between the best-seller and high-brow has been finally demolished by his works. His novels are highly entertaining and, at the same time, very slick, real and sophisticated. His publication figure has literally reached over a million copies for each work and that remains a milestone for Indian English novel. The present dissertation analyses Chetan Bhagat's novels thematically and stylistically to discover the secret of his immense success. He closely resembles Vikram Seth in his iconoclastic irreverence for the holy cows of traditional India. His characters are not ready to offer simple conformism. They are social rebels who remind us of the angry young men. His novels are not set in the laid-back milieu of small-town India; they are right in the hustle and bustle of Metropolitan Indian cities where life moves at a fast pace and change is preferred to continuity.

Chetan Bhagat's first book, *Five Point Someone-What Not to Do at IIT* (May 2004) is a novel about three boys who join IIT Delhi and try to cope with the notoriously heavy workload of the institute. This book has continued to stay on the *India Today* best-seller list ever since its publication (190 weeks in January, 2008). It won him the Society Young Achiever's award in 2004 and the Publisher's Recognition award in 2005.

The novel is set in the Indian Institute of Technology, Delhi, in the period 1991 to 1995. It is about the adventures of three mechanical engineering students (and friends), Hari Kumar (the narrator), Ryan Oberoi, and Alok Gupta, who fail to cope with the grading system of the IITs and come to be known as five pointers due to their perennially low 5 points something GPA's.

The book is narrated in the first person by Hari, with some small passages by his friends Ryan and Alok, as well as a letter by Hari's girlfriend Neha Cherian. It deals with the lives of the three friends whose elation on making it to one of the best engineering colleges in India is quickly deflated by the rigor and monotony of academic work. Most of the book deals with the numerous attempts by the trio to cope with and/or beat the system as well as Hari's fling with Neha who just happens to be the daughter of Prof. Cherian, the domineering head of the Mechanical Engineering Department.

While the tone of the novel is humorous, it takes some dark turns every now and then, especially when it comes to the families of the main characters. Most of the action, however, takes place inside the campus as the boys, led by the ever creative Ryan, frequently keep lamenting how the internationally lauded IIT system has stifled their creativity by forcing them to value grades more than anything else. Uninspiring teaching and numerous assignments add to their woes although the boys do find a sympathizer in Prof. Veera, the new fluid mechanics professor.

It is difficult to say if the book is romantically science or scientifically romance. But the best part is that it is scientifically vulgar!

One Night @ the Call Center or *ON@CC* is Chetan Bhagat's second novel, first published in 2005. The novel revolves around a group of six call center employees working in Connexions Call Center in the Delhi suburb of Gurgaon in Haryana. It is filled with a lot of drama with unpleasant things happening to all of the leading characters. The story takes a dramatic and decisive turn when they get a phone call from God. The story begins with a train journey from Kanpur to Delhi. During the journey, the author meets a very beautiful girl. The girl offers to tell the author a story on the condition that he has to make it his second book. After a lot of hesitation, the author agrees. Claimed to be based on a true story, the author chooses a person named Shyam Mehra (alias Sam Marcy) as the protagonist who is one among the six call center employees featured. He is the narrator of the story. He lives in Gurgaon, Haryana with his parents. He is portrayed as an average Joe, someone who can be easily related with. His ex-girlfriend Priyanka works in the same call center as he does. He loves her even after breaking up and is quite frequently shown dreaming about the good and bad times that he spent with her. One of the reasons for his break-up was that

Priyanka's mother did not approve of Shyam as she felt that in order to wed her daughter, Shyam should at least be a team leader. Shyam tries hard to become a team leader, but his current manager, Bakshi, dissapproves of him on the contention that Shyam is not a go-getter. Shyam feels that Bakshi is a poor boss, yet he continues to work for lack of options. Shyam works with Vroom on a Troubleshooting Website, a project that he hopes would showcase his capabilities to be Team Leader. He is confused as he doesn't know who he hates more—his boss Bakshi or Priyanka's mother. However, after getting a phone-call from God, he gains in confidence, takes his revenge on Bakshi and wins over the love of his life, Priyanka.

One of the salient features of this novel is that all the characters featuring in this novel have a dramatic and disturbing event during the night when they receive a call from God. Shyam is very upset to learn that Priyanka is engaged to a person called Ganesh Gupta, who works at Microsoft in the U.S. To add to his woes, he is horrified to learn that Bakshi had cheated him, and Vroom, by submitting the Troubleshooting Website to the Boston centre as his own without crediting himself and Vroom. Priyanka is first happy when she is engaged to Ganesh Gupta, who works for Microsoft; but becomes furious when she hears that her parents have planned her marriage the very next month, which she feels is too early. Both her mother and Ganesh press her to agree to this proposal. She is even more saddened by the fact that Shyam was eavesdropping on her conversation with Ganesh. When Vroom and Shyam show her that Ganesh had forged his pictures to hide his baldness, she disapproves Ganesh for having cheated her. Esha had earlier done a compromise by sleeping with a designer to get a modeling contract. However, the guy turned out to be opportunistic as he betrays her by telling that she can't become a model due to her height. He also tries to console her by sending her some money. Esha feels terribly betrayed and tries to suppress the mental pain by inflicting herself with physical pain by purposely cutting her skin. Vroom is shocked to learn that Bakshi has cheated him and Shyam by submitting their work as his own. To add to his miseries, he overhears Esha telling the other girls that she had slept with a designer to get a modeling contract. Radhika, who loved her husband very much, is shocked to learn about his dark side. When Vroom calls up her husband portraying as a Radio Jockey and asks him to dedicate roses and a song to someone special, he chooses his girlfriend, Payal, over his wife. Radhika who listens to this gets terribly upset as her husband has betrayed her. Military Uncle tries to be nice to his son and grandson. But when he sends some pictures via mail to his grandson, his son loses his cool and asks him to beep out of his life. This leaves Military Uncle heartbroken.

The phone call from God is one of the salient features in the novel. The author has represented God as a friendly figure rather than a boss. He is shown as speaking in modern English rather than the stereotypical pure English or Latin that one usually encounters God speaking. The circumstances in which the characters of the novel get a phone call from God have already been discussed. In order to cheer themselves up, all the lead characters of the novel decide to go and enjoy at a night club. After enjoying for a while, they leave for office. Midway through the journey, Vroom starts to feel nauseated after drinking alcohol and so they stop and venture out. Vroom throws up and also breaks the window-pane of a shop thus spreading an alarm. They rush out of the place in fear. While returning, they face a life-threatening situation when their Qualis crashes into a construction site hanging over a mesh of iron construction rods. As the rods begin to yield slowly, they start to panic. They are unable to call for help as there is no mobile phone network at that place. In this situation, Shyam's mobile phone starts ringing. The phone call is from God. He speaks to all of them and gives them suggestions to improve their life. After that, God also advises them on how to get their vehicle out of the construction site. The conversation with God motivates the group to such an extent that they all plan together to teach their boss a lesson, to improve the call center's business and go after what they wanted.

The 3 Mistakes of My Life is the third novel written by Chetan Bhagat. The novel was published in May 2008 and had an initial print-run of 200000. The novel follows the story of three friends and is based in the city of Ahmedabad in Western India. It set in the year 2000, when a young boy in Ahmedabad called Govind dreams of starting a business, and is based on real events. To accommodate his friends Ishaan and Omi's passion, they open a cricket shop. However, each has a different motive: Govind's goal is to make money; Ishaan desires to nurture Ali, a gifted batsman; Omi just wants to be with his friends. During the story the characters have to deal with religious politics, earthquake, riots, unacceptable love and their own mistakes. The central consciousness in the novel, Govind, is an ordinary guy with which anybody can relate. He has very few desires but he is obsessed with the ambition to make it big. His main ambition is to become a businessman. His best friends are Omi and Ish. He also loves Vidya. Govind does not quite believe in God and is an agnostic. Friendship, business and mathematics are the most important things of his life. He is the narrator of this story. Ishaan is a big cricket freak and also a patriot at heart. Ishaan has been the best cricketer in his locality and school. He helps Govind's business by organising daily cricket coaching camps. He has a family which makes life worse for him. His father constantly nags him and his mother worsens the situation by keeping quiet. He has a younger sister, Vidya about whom he is quite protective. Omi is the son of the Hindu priest of the local temple. His family enjoys great respect among the people. He is a bit dumb kinda boy and has not many dreams, but likes to concentrate on having a healthy body. However, he resents growing up and being a saint like his father. He is a religious person and actively takes part in his maternal uncle's (Bittoo Mama) religious politics. He is however confused about his religious views which are mainly influenced by Bittoo Mama. Vidya is Ishaan's sister. She is a rebel at heart and dreams to break free from the constraints of a typical middle-class family and society, to go to Mumbai and do a course in PR and be independent. She however despises maths which is required for her medical entrance exams. Hence, Ish asks Govind to take her maths tuition. However, in between their tuition they fall in love, have intimate sexual relations, which is unaccepted by anyone. Only Omi figures out the relationship Govind and Vidya share and also reminds Govind about the consequenes of Ish getting to know about it. Ali is a student in Ish's coaching classes and a great cricketer because of a rare nature's gift. However, he doesn't play too much cricket as he gets tired really fast and enjoys playing marbles. He is Muslim boy and respects Ish like a Guru. He too, like Ish is patriotic at heart. He denies the offer of an Australian scholarship and wants to play in the Indian side. Bitto Mama is the maternal uncle of Omi and belongs to a Hindu political Party. He follows the preachings of Parekh-ji, a political-cum-spiritual leader and has complete faith in him. He has locked his horns with Ali's father who belongs to the Secular Party. He has a son Dhiraj and he is not fond of Govind as he is an agnostic. He is the main antagonist of the story. *The 3 Mistakes of My Life* highlights the dangerous mix of religion, politics, and economics that is the hallmark of contemporary India.

Chetan's latest fictional work, *2 States* (2009) is by his own admission a thinly veiled accont of his own love affair and marriage. The central fable is the love and wooing of Ananya, a Tamil Brahmin girl, by Krish, a North Indian Punjabi boy. They meet at IIM, Ahmedabad and get along very well, before the family and cultural differences interfere to rock their boat. The problem area in *2 States* is regionalism that causes huge misunderstandings between Punjabis and Madrasis (Tamilians). The denoument is a victory of One India Concept over divisive forces of regionalism. Chetan Bhagat has said about this work:

> *2 States* is the story of my marriage and I have dedicated the book to my in-laws. I think this is the first time any Indian writer has dedicated a book to his in-laws', he said 'The book is funny and completely different from *Five Point Someone,One Night@the Call Center* and *3 Mistakes*. I did not want to write about friends any more'. Bhagat said *2 States* is about Krish and Ananya, who are from two different states of India. They are deeply in love and want to get married. But their parents do not agree. To convert the

> love story into a wedding, the couple have a tough fight ahead of them. 'Indian love marriages are not easy. It's not just the boy and the girl who fall in love. Everyone—both their clans—have to fall in love. In the end, the boy and girl start questioning whether there's anyting more left to it and even fight. But it's important—at least for me—what parents think of your marriage,' Bhagat said. (*Net-entry*)[11]

My hypothesis about Chetan Bhagat's fiction, that I hope to prove through sufficient illustrations from his texts, is that his works touch an emotional chord in the new emerging Metro-Generation in India. His Metro-Fiction shows the dreams and hopes of an aggressively ambitious generation whose laughter is tinged with tears. His characters are irreverent young people whose motto in life its—Get going or Get out of the way. Yet there remains a poll of gloom about these bright young people, an existential angst about their future and an unrelenting presence of their past. This curious blend of humour and pathos, of hopes and fears, of success and failure marks his best-selling dark comedies of contemporary India.

Notes

1. Q.D. Leavis: *Collected Essays* (Vol. I) (London, Chatto & Windus, 1970) pp. 10-11 (Emphasis added).
2. John Fernes: 'Q.D. Leavis Criticism: The Human Core' *Modern Age,* Spring 2003, p. 170.
3. Arnold Kettle: *An Introduction to English Novel (Vol.* II) (Delhi, Universal, 1990), p. 60.
4. P.H. Furbank: 'The Twentieth Century Best Seller' in *Pelican Guide to English Literature,* Vol. VII, (Harmondsworth, Penguin, 1964). p. 429.
5. Vide, P.H. Furbank, p. 429.
6. P.H. Furbank, p. 432.
7. P.H. Furbank, p. 432.
8. Kenneth Allsop: *The Angry Decade* (London, MacMillan, 1966). p. 9 (Emphasis added)
9. Vide, Arnold Kettle, p. 176.
10. Vikram Seth: *A Suitable Boy* (Delhi, Penguin Books, 1993), p. 815.
11. http://timesofindia.indiatimes.com/city/bangalore/22.11.2009

Five Point Someone: The Metro Generation Under Pressure of Expectations

2

The contours of a best-seller, as analyzed in the first chapter, are well-defined. It is a work of fiction highly accessible to a large number of the reading public, not only commercially but also intellectually. The author keeps a fair distance from unrequired erudition, needless allusions and high-sounding words. He has a story to tell and he does so in a neat, racy style with ladle-full of youth lingo and techie-words. Secondly, he refuses to preach and advise about traditions and archetypal totems. Rather, he attacks the holy cows of society with infectious energy. Thirdly, he focuses more on emotional drama rather than on polemics or debates; his pen unburdened of past regrets or future fears. Fourthly, the author of a best-seller needs to find the pulse of the youth, to locate a theme near the young hearts, and to communicate on a wave-length that reaches out far and wide.

On all these counts Chetan Bhagat's debut novel, *Five Point Someone* (2004), scores a perfect ten. It takes up the theme of disoriented youth in a renowned academic campus that puts a premium on conformism and rote-learning, and discourages any hint of innovation or rebellion. The GPA(Grade Point Average) scores hang like a sword of Damocles on youthful heads, and any score around five is like a blot on the scutcheon, a perpetual question mark about the academic abilities of the student. The Five-Pointer is dehumanized, rejected as an outcast not worthy of being identified. He is a back-bencher, a loser, an object of pity and humour at the same time. The story brutally exposes the psychological maiming of the unfortunate Five-Pointers; a trauma that leads to neurosis and suicidal alienation.

As Bhagat's first novel, Five Point Someone contains a large chunk of his autobiography; his own experiences as an under-achiever at Indian Institute of Technology, New Delhi. Yet he never talks like a grumbling loser, rather he seems to celebrate the freedom that being unburdened of great expectations provides. That he is not writing only about himself but his own young generation is proved by his careful choice of dramatis personae. Hari, the narrator, is a plump middle class boy, obviously the authore's self-portrait. The second boy in the gang is Ryan Oberai, a rebellious brat from a swanky noveau riche family, with prestigious public school background and undisputed qualities of heart and mind. The third boy is Alok, an awkward, bespectacled, stunted youngster from a poor family, who looks at IIT as a key to his financial emancipation. Thus the core group of players presents in microcosm the whole set-up of a Metro society from the filthy rich to the marginalized poor, so that each class of the readers can somehow empathise with the lead actors. This widening of the base shows Chetan Bhagat's sheer brilliance in planning and executing his attempt to create a best-seller.

Five Point Someone: What Not to Do at IIT, begins with a disclaimer:

> BEFORE I REALLY BEGIN THIS BOOK, LET ME FIRST TELL you what this book is not. It is not a guide on how to live through college. On the contrary, it is probably an example of how screwed up your college years can get if you don't think straight.[1]

Later Chetan Bhagat said in an interview that his novel is all about bonding, not GPA, at IIT. Score nine on ten and have, no one eating paranthas with you; score five and have someone who does. Five and a friend is better than 10 and a vacuum.[2]

Hari, Ryan and Alok make it to the IIT Delhi. But can they cope with the pressure of their studies? The initial trauma for them is the ragging which is a part of India's elite colleges and universities. Alok and Hari submit to their humiliation:

> 'No talking!' Baku said, one scrawny hand up. 'No talking, just remove those damn clothes.'
>
> Another demon grinned at us, slapping his bare stomach every few seconds. There seemed to be no choice so we surrendered every item of our clothing, shivering at the unholy glee in Baku's face as he walked by each of us, checking us out and grinning.
>
> Nakedness made the difference between our bodies more stark as Alok and me drew figures on the floor with deeply embarrassed toes, trying to be casual about our twisted balloon figures. Ryan's body was flawless, man, he was a hunk; muscles that cut at the right places and a body frame that for once resembled the human body shown in biology books. You could describe his body as sculpture. Alok and I, on the other hand, weren't exactly what you'd call art.
>
> (*Five Point*, 3-4)

But Ryan is different. He puts up with his tormentors for a while, but then he hits back with a vengeance:

> 'Sir, stop,' Ryan said, in a louder voice.
>
> 'Fuck off,' Baku dismissed, disbelief writ large in his widened eyes at this blatant rebellion against his age-old authority.
>
> As Baku put the bottles in position, Ryan abandoned his pin-up pose and jumped. Catching him unawares, he grabbed the two bottles and stamped hard on Baku's feet. Baku released his hands and the bottles were with Ryan, James Bond style.
>
> We knew that stomp hurt since Baku's scream was ultrasonic.
>
> 'Get this bastard,' Baku shrieked in agony.
>
> (*Five Point*, 5)

This is the beginning of friendship among this unlikely trio of *losers*. Ryan assumes a heroic image in the eyes of Hari and Alok and they choose to follow his lead:

> Ryan's heroics were enough to make us all bond faster than *Fevicol*. Besides, we were hostelite neighbours and in the same engineering department. They say you should not get into a relationship with people you sleep with on the first date. Well, though we hadn't slept together, we had seen each other naked at the primary meet, so perhaps we should have refrained from striking up a friendship. But our troika was kind of inevitable.
>
> (*Five Point*, 7) (Emphasis added)

The bond of love between the three lasts the ups and downs of life in the IIT. Hari is fat, confused about sticking to books, likes a professor's daughter, and wants to be Ryan. Ryan is good-looking, confident, drinks and gets others to drink vodka, has parents abroad and curiously stashes away letters from there. Alok is fat, his father's ill, sister unmarried, family can't make ends meet-he wants to make 9 on 10. This is the trouble: Alok likes time with both, but his own too, to make the grades; Hari partly goes with Alok, but likes to mimic Ryan; Ryan loves pop music, smoke joints and vodka. Time for oneself to make it big and time together for fun: that is the dilemma of choice for all three of them.

Alok and Hari give into Ryan. They talk shop, flirt a bit, crack jokes on gals they'd love to be with but can't, drink vodka on the insti roof, and guess what, mess up the quiz, land GPAs below six. At IIT, it means you are a nothing.

The quiz disaster happens in Chapter II. The troika realizes that if they skewer the IIT system, it comes back to double screw them. Before they know it they are relegated as back-benchers, a set of losers. While their families wanted them to conquer the world, they are struggling to survive. This is what happens:

> Prof. Sen wrote the customary summary scores on the blackboard.

> *Average*: 11/20
>
> *High*: 17/20
>
> *Low*: 3/20
>
> He kept those written for a few minutes, before proceeding with his Lecture on cantilever beams.
>
> "I have the lowest. Did you see that?" Ryan whispered to me, unmoved by cantilever beams. It was hard to figure out what he was feeling at this point. Even thouh he was trying to stay calm and expressionless, I could tell he was having trouble digesting his result. He re-read his quiz, it did not change the score.
>
> Alok was in a different orbit. His face looked like it had on ragging day. He viewed the answer sheet like he had the coke bottle, an expression of anxiety mixed with sadness. It's in these moments that Alok is most vulnerable, you nudge him just a little bit and you know he'd cry. But for now, the quiz results were a repulsive enough sight.
>
> I saw my own answer sheet. The instructor had written my score in big but careless letters, like graffiti written with contempt. Now I am no Einstein or anything, but this never happened to me in school. My score was five on twenty, or twenty-five per cent; I had never in my life scored less than three times as much. Ouch, the first quiz in IIT hurt.
>
> But take Ryan's scores. I wondered if it had been worth it for him to even study last night. I was two points ahead of him, or wait a minute, sixty-six per cent ahead of him, that made me feel better. Thank god for relative misery!
>
> (*Five Point*, 20)

One miscalculation has caused the quiz disaster. The evening before they had gone for fun. To get away from their blues, the three rode pillion on Ryan's ramshackle scooter to see a sci-fi film, The Terminator. But once they come back, they get the super-secret information of the next day being scheduled for a surprise quiz. The spectre of failure comes back to haunt them throughout their subsequent days at the IIT. The first semester results brand them as loser:

> 'THEY'RE OUT!' ALOK SAID, SHAKING RYAN'S SHOULDER on a Saturday morning as if India had won the World Cup or nude women were rolling on the grass outside. 'The major results are out!'
>
> 'I want to sleep?' Ryan said, burrowing deeper under the quilt that Alok eventually succeeded in tugging off.
>
> We reached the institute where a crowd of students had gathered to see their first set of grades. From these one could determine their first grade point average, or GPA, on the 10 point scale. The topper would be close to 10.00, while the average would be around 6.50. We, however, were closer to the bottom. Clicking through the scientfic calculator, Alok calculated our scores.
>
> 'Ok, Hari is at 5.46 and...Ryan is at 5.01 and I...I'm at 5.88', Alok said.
>
> 'So all of us are five-pointers,' I said, as if making a particularly insightful comment.
>
> 'Congrats Alok, you have topped amongst us,' Ryan said.
>
> Topped amongst us, I thought. As if we were the high-brain society or something. These were pathetic grades: we ranked in the high 200s in a class of 300 students. Alok recalculated his score, hoping for some miracle to happen on the calculator. But miracles never happen at IIT, only crap grades do.
>
> *(Five Point,* 60-61) (Emphasis added)

However, the novel is not a lament of failure. It also brings out the humour, adventure and sheer brilliance of performance at the IIT. Ryan is the one rebel to take on the system, to upset the applecart of tradition and conformism. In an encounter early in the novel he takes on Prof. Dubey who explains what a machine is:

> 'Shshh,' ordered Prof. Dubey, looking at the three of us, 'anyway, the definition of a machine is simple. It is

> anything that reduces human effort. Anything. So, see the world around you and it is full of machines.'
>
> (*Five Point*, 9)

The whole class agrees without a whimper. But Ryan has a question that has the professor stumped:

> A feeling of collective joy darted through the class for having managed to convert Prof. Dubey's sour expression into smiles.
>
> 'Sir, what about a gym machine, like a bench press or something?' Ryan interrupted the bonhomie.
>
> 'What about it?' Prof. Dubey stopped beaming.
>
> 'That doesn't reduce human effort. In fact, it increases it.'
>
> The class fell silent again.
>
> 'Well, I mean...' Prof. Dubey said as he scouted for arguments.
>
> Boy, did Ryan really have a point?
>
> 'Perhaps it is too simple a definition then?' Ryan said in a pseudo-helpful voice.
>
> 'What are you trying to do?' the professor asked tight-lipped as he came close to us again, 'Are you saying that I am wrong?'
>
> 'No Sir, I'm just...'
>
> 'Watch it son. In my class, just watch it,' was all Prof. Dubey said as he moved to the front.
>
> (*Five Point*, 10-11)

Having no rational answer to Ryan's question, the professor resorts to threats and coercion. Rebellion has to be crushed at any cost. He warns the class:

> 'That is it for today. Best of luck once again for your stay here. Remember, as your head of department Prof. Cherian says, the tough workload is by design, to keep you on your toes. And respect the grading system. You get bad grades, and I assure you-you get no job, no school and no future. If you do well, the world is your

> oyster. So, don't slip, not even once, or there will be no oyster, just slush.'
>
> A shiver ran through all of us as with that quote the professor slammed the duster on the desk and walked away in a cloud of chalk.
>
> (*Five Points,* 11) (Emphasis added)

In just a few months Ryan has seen through the system. He realizes that IIT is only a place for muggers; no individual voice is heard with respect if it has something new or original to offer. He says regretfully:

> But Ryan had more. 'This system of relative grading and over-burdening the students. I mean it kills the best fun years of your life. But it kills something else. Where is the room for original thought? Where is the time for creativity? It is not fair?' (*Five Point,* 98) (Emphasis added)

Later he works out with his friends a scheme on how to beat the system. He calls it C2D, (*Cooperate to Dominate*). In the method the three will divide the work load and attend classes accordingly. Later they will copy out assignments from each-other. But before presenting his plans he tells others about the lousy system at the IIT that he cells a *mice-race.*

> 'And this IIT system is nothing but a mice race. It is not a rat race, mind you, as rats sound somewhat shrewd and clever. So it is not about that. It is about mindlessly running a race for four years, in every class, every assignment and every test. It is a race where Profs. judge you every ten steps, with a GPA stamped on you every semester. Profs. who have no idea what science and learning are about. Yes, that is what I think of the profs. I mean, what have IITs given to this country? Name one invention in the last three decades...
>
> ...screw the profs. Coming back, this system is an unfair race. If you are a mouse who thinks or pauses to make friends with other runners, or stops to figure out what you want to do in life, or drag baggage from the

> past, then you will be pushed behind. As we have been pushed behind by morons like Venkat.
>
> (*Five Point,* 101) (Emphasis added)

After this tirade he comes out with his plan to fight against this unfair system. This way they will cheat by copying rather than learn for themselves. He says:

> 'So, what is with the implementation of the theory? How does that work?' I spoke idly.
>
> 'C2D,' Ryan said.
>
> 'What the hell is that?' It sounded like a code in those damn sci–fi movies.
>
> 'Cooperate?' Ryan said and fell on his bed, only half-intentionally.
>
> 'Cooperate?'
>
> 'Yes, Cooperate to Dominate, C2D...' Ryan said and closed his eyes. All that work for the party and the vodka had taken their toll. He had passed out.
>
> 'Come, fellow mouse, Let's go to our room,' Alok said.
>
> The party was over.
>
> (*Five Point,* 105) (Emphasis added)

Desperate, at the end of their tether, Ryan and friends decide to steal the term paper from Prof. Cherian's room. When they are caught red-handed their career is in serious trouble. They are hauled up before the Disco, the disciplinary committee. The narrator can crack a joke even this darkest hour. He remembers:

> THE IIT DISCO IS ABOUT AS FAR AWAY FROM DANCING AS it can get. Here the lighting is dull, the room dead silent and almost everyone elderly. Around ten Profs. sat around a semi-circular table, while the accused students were bang in the centre. Profs. fire questions at students from all directions, the location placing us at minimum distance to each one of them. It is essentially a more efficient design of a courtroom, I guess, Indem-inspired.
>
> (*Five Point*, 203)

The rest of the novel shows how the boys are rusticated for one semester and how Ryan saves their career with his hard lab work and the kindness of Prof. Veera. Veera is one ideal teacher who encourages research and innovation of Ryan by hiring him as his assistant and unlocking the doors of his career. The novel ends with the careers of the boys somewhat settled and their parting on a note of sorrow and new hope.

Concurrently in the background runs a love story between Hari and Neha, daughter of Prof. Cherian. The point of the story is to highlight Neha's loneliness, as her brother, Sameer, had committed suicide. The reason was that he could not qualify to enter the IIT as his father, Cherian, wanted. Neha keeps this secret to herself but one day her father reads the suicide note and is broken. He realizes that every boy cannot be an engineer. The whole theme of IIT and the youth is summed up in a Convocation address that is only a dream of the narrator, Hari. Hari believes that Prof. Cherian is talking to his students at the passing out day:

> 'Once upon a time there was a student at IIT. He was very bright, and this is true, his GPA was 10.00 after four years. He didn't have a lot of friends, as to keep such a high GPA, you only have so much time for friends.'
>
> 'But he did have classmates. Classmates who this bright boy thought were less smart than him, classmates who were selfish and wanted to make the most money or go to the USA with minimum effort. And the classmates did exactly that. They went to work for multinationals and some went abroad. Some of them opened their own companies in the USA–mostly in computers and software. This was twenty years ago mind you, so computers were a very new thing.'...
>
> 'So our bright boy was disappointed. He still kept trying but apart from being a Professor, there isn't much one could achieve here. Ten years passed, when his friends from college visited home. One of them had a GPA of seven point something, and he had own

software company. The turnover had reached two hundred million dollars. Another friend was heading a toothpaste MNC, and came in a BMW. Of course, this didn't bother the principled bright boy. Or so he thought.

'As you guessed, that bright boy was me. And at that time I thought it didn't matter if others had achieved more personally. I was still the one with the better GPA, the smarter one, the brighter one. Somehow, on that day, I decided my son must get into IIT. I wanted him to carry on my family's strong intellectual tradition. Strong intellectual tradition—that is what I called it. But it was just my big ego. My son wanted to be a lawyer, hated maths. I hated him for hating maths. I pushed him just as I pushed students in my class. He failed to get in the first time and I made life hell for him. He failed a second time and I made his life an even bigger hell. Then he failed to get in the third time. And this time, he killed himself…

'And that is when I realized that GPAs make a good student, but not a good person. We judge people here by their GPA. If you are a nine, you are the best. If you are a five, you are useless. I used to despise the low GPAs so much that when Ryan submitted a research proposal on lubricants, I judged it without even reading it.

But these boys have something really promising. I saw the proposal the second time. I can tell you, any investor who invests in this will earn a rainbow...

'You all know that I have a daughter. But I also had a son, who died in a rail track accident five years ago. At that time, we thought it was an accident. But this...' Cherian said as he pulled out Samir's letter, 'is my son's letter I got only a few weeks ago. He wrote this to my daughter on the day he died. He killed himself because he did not get into IIT. He killed himself because of me,' Cherian said and paused for a long time. He removed his spectacles and wiped his eyes.

> The audience was silent enough to hear Cherian's mild sobs....
>
> 'Anyway, this is my message to all you students as you find your future. One, believe in yourself, and don't let a GPA, performance review or promotion in a job define you. There is more to life than these things-your family, your friends, your internal desires and goals. And the grades you get in dealing with each of these areas will define you as a person.
>
> Two, don't judge others too quickly. I thought my son was useless because he didn't get into IIT. I tell you what, I was a useless father. It is great to get into IIT, but it is not the end of the world if you don't. ALL of you should be proud to have the IIT tag, but never ever judge anyone who is not from this institute-that alone can define the greatness of this institute....
>
> 'And last don't take yourself too seriously. We professors are to be blamed even more for this. Life is too short, enjoy yourself to the fullest. One of the best parts of campus life is the friends you make. And make sure you make them for life. Yes, I have heard the stories. Sometimes I wish I had had a friend, even if that meant a lower GPA. It must be good to have vodka on top of the institute roof at night.'
>
> (*Five Point*, 261-65) (Emphasis added)

The last part of this monologue brings us to the heart of the novel. *Five Point Someone* is not a UGC report on the failures of the IIT. For this Chetan Bhagat may have written a column as he later did for *The Times of India.*

> The cycle perpetuates itself, and we continue to create a second-rate society of followers rather than change-embracing leaders. I have hope that the current generation will break this norm and start questioning the great Indian way. I have hope that the current HRD minister will acknowledge this problem and do something. I have hope that Indians will start questioning any politician they meet on what they are

> doing about the education system at every place possible. I have hope that people will realise that making new state universities. Maybe I am right, maybe my hope is justified and maybe I will live to see the change. Or maybe I've got it all wrong, my optimism is misplaced and I am just, as they say, one of the idiots.[3]

Five Point Someone is a novel, not about IIT, but about love and friendship. It is a *Bildungsroman*, a coming of age story involving Hari, his friends and his girlfriend. It is a *black comedy* packed with action, dialogue, fun and some sex. It is about bonding in hostel rooms, at road-side dhabas, and on insti-roof. It is about vodka and Pink Floyd, about marijuana and hand-holding. Have a look at this scene:

> He changed the tape and put on another Pink Floyd. I saw the levels of the vodka bottle drop and Ryan scrapping through his brown bag for the last joint of the day. A half-moon lit up the sky, and bright little stars looked smug, winking down at us like students with higher GPAs.
>
> You know the thing about Floyd? Not only are they damn good they sound better with every drink, like the singers designed them for alcohol. Like samosas-chutney, idli-sambhar or rajma-chawal, Floyd and vodka are in a combo-class of their own.
>
> (*Five Point,* 81) (Emphasis added)

The eating out, wandering around and occasional films are the spice of life at the IIT. The troika has great fun in spite of their low GPA's. And above all there is dedicated friendship. Ryan fights for his friends and does all to save their lives and careers. His labour saves them from disgrace and loss of term:

> The three of us were in our common study room one day, copying Alok's thermal science assignment.
>
> 'So, Prof. Vohra is mad at you now,' Alok said.
>
> Ryan kept silent.
>
> 'Of course he would be. You should have seen his face,' I contributed.

> Alok laughed, shaking his head.
>
> 'He can flunk me for all I care,' Ryan stated.
>
> 'That is not the point,' Alok began.
>
> 'Fatso, you won't get the point, so give up. By the way, Prof Veera called me to talk about my lubricant assignment.'
>
> 'Really?' Alok and I said in unison, wondering if Prof Veera had caught us cheating.
>
> 'Nothing to worry guys. I gave him a separate paper, it wasn't a class assignment.'
>
> 'You have time to do separate papers?' I said.
>
> 'I have time to do what I want. I had thought on doing some experiments with various substance mixtures to check lubricant efficiency in a scooter engine.'
>
> (*Five Point*, 119)

Then there is the love between Hari and Neha. Their sexual closeness is a high voltage drama in the novel:

> I curled up next to her and held her. She turned her face towards me, almost in reflex. We kissed, and then we kissed again. Then she held my hand and did something that she had never done before; she put it on her breast.
>
> Wow, my head went into a tizzy. What happened to this girl? Had she lost her mind? I certainly lost mine and forgot about operation Pendulum.
>
> My hand slid under her T-shirt and then clumsily under the bra. Life would be so much better without books.
>
> 'Easy Tiger easy,' she said. I liked it that she called me Tiger.
>
> She sat up to remove her T-shirt. And then the rest. I sat there transfixed, trying hard not to let my tongue hang loose and pant like a dog.
>
> 'Well Tiger, are you going to remove anything or not?' she said.

> 'I...I...' I said as she pulled me close.
>
> Half an hour later, we lay on the bed, spent but completely content. I looked up at the old ceiling fan in Neha's room, going around in awkward circles and felt dizzy with happiness.
>
> 'So? Neha said.
>
> 'So what,' I said, regaining my equilibrium...
>
> 'Yeah, right. Here I am, lying naked with a man who was drunk in his viva, while my Dad is less than a kilometer away in his office,' she said and laughed, 'It's so liberating.'
>
> (*Five Point*, 168-69)

And after this love-making he goes out to buy fags in Cherian's shirt in his Maruti 800, when Cherian meets him on the street. It is pure *slop-stich comedy.*

> 'What happened?' Alok asked as he came to Ryan's room.
>
> 'Hell. Hell happened.' I regained my pulse and related the whole story.
>
> Ryan started laughing. Even though he is bold and everything, that is not what I expected from him. Cherian was there, holding my bloody collar and threatening to ruin me.
>
> 'Fuck Ryan, this is not funny,' I said.
>
> 'Oh really,' he said, laughing even harder, 'then what is it? Cherian's shirt, Neha in a bedsheet. Prof. must have gone psycho,' Ryan paused to laugh some more. 'I wish I was there.' 'Shut up. This is added tension man,' Alok said.
>
> (*Five Point,* 176) (Emphasis added)

Five Point Someone is a best-seller because it exposes the lousy system that operates in Indian colleges and universities; thus finding an echo in every young heart that has ached during the relentless pressure of examinations. But more than that it has succeeded in expressing the sheer exuberance of youth; the misty days of friendship and love, first love; the sepia-tone memories of hard-nosed teachers and students bunking classes to go to the canteen or a movie-hall. The sheer nostalgia of those bitter-sweet campus days has connected Chetan Bhagat to his young audience who cannot have enough of his twangy prose. His choice of words and imagery is in line with the Metro lingo with profusion of f.... words, and abbreviations like insti, prof, fatso or cog that connect his work to the net-savvy generation.

The novel stands out because the ambience is unusual, characters are close to genuine and incidents oscillate between real and absurd. Bhagat intelligently takes every engineering student down the memory lane. Situations might not have been the same for every one; nevertheless, like Hari wishes to be Ryan, even for the nine pointers the narrated lives of *Five Point Someone* would have been a wish unfulfilled.

Chetan Bhagat's captivating, hilarious and breezy debut novel Five Point Someone about life on a college campus, has not only garnerd rave reviews but also become a national best-seller. In March 2008, *New York Times* called him the biggest selling English author in India's history.

Chetan is driven by passion to write and he is a good story teller. The characters are believable and one can easily relate to them. The novel tugs at your heartstrings and has resonated well with young Indian readers, (the can-do generation) and especially with all those who have lived on Indian college campuses, sharing their dreams, aspirations and anxieties with fellow students from diverse backgrounds. Chetan does not moralize in his novels. Admittedly prestigious institutions like IIT's are highly competitive but the mice race to get top grades, and high-salaried jobs needs to be debated. Creativity, thinking out-of-the-box needs to be encouraged. And there ought to be room for bit of fun too!

How Chetan planned and wrote his debut novel, *Five Point Someone,* can be finally put into perspective with reference to an interview that is available on his website. The interview dates back to early 2004:

Q. What is *Five Point Someone* about?

A. *Five Point Someone* is about three boys in IIT who can't cope with the system. Their poor grade point average, brands them as the underperformers of IIT, society and tests everything else they hold important—friends, love, dreams and responsibilities. How important are grades or broadly speaking, how important is success compared to other aspects of your life? *Five Point Someone* explores this question.

Q. Wow, sounds heavy. Is it?

A. Oh No! Not at all. The primary idea of this book is to entertain the reader. The genre is humour, and it attempts to bring the reader back into their college days where money was scarce, frends were plenty and even when facing deep life issues—you were having fun.

Q. Tell us something more about the writing style used in the book.

A. The writing style is extremely informal. This may be referred to as modern English, but the idea is to write as people talk in college age. Hence, no flowery language, no tough words you dreaded in a dictation, no set rules. Yet—it works, because it is the language of real people.

Q. How big is the book?

A. The final details are being worked out, but expected to be around 250 pages which is a medium sized novel. However, because of the simple language, the book reads much faster.

Q. So the book is set in IIT?

A. Yes, the book is set in the IIT Delhi campus. Loctions, places and venues are all very real. And the prices for paranthas are real too—though at one point in time in the past.

Q. Can we know a bit more about the story?

A. Hmmm. Telling you too much will take away something. Let us just say three guys Hari, Alok and

Ryan are wingmates in the hostel and have the same department. The three of them become the best friends, but they have different personalities, and different expectations out of the future. They have a rough start, and the downward spiral of the IIT system grips them before they know it. Does that help?

Q. Sort of. And what is the love angle in the book?

A. There is one female character in the book, the beautiful Neha, daughter of Professor Cherian. Rest, when you pick.[5]

It is no surprise that Chetan Bhagat's debut novel has been adapted to create a hugely successful Hindi movie, 3 idiots. There has been a credits controversy surrounding the screen-play of the film, but that issue is not relevant to this study. The fact remains that a best-seller has been converted into a mega box-office success, about five years after its publication. This simply proves that Chetan Bhagat's novel has passed the test of time, one of the tests prescribed by Longinus in his evaluation of good literature. From a best-seller, the novel has graduated into a steady-seller.

Notes

1. Chetan Bhagat: *Five Point Someone* (Delhi, Rupa, 2004 Rpt. 2008) p.1. (All subsequent citations are from this edition and the page no's have been given in parenthesis)
2. 'Five Points, paranthas, and some friends' *The Hindu*, Tuesday, May 25.2004
3. Chetan Bhagat: 'The Indian Institute of Idiots' *The Times of India*, Delhi; December, 2009 p. 14. (Emphasis added)
4. Net entry: www.chetanbhagat.com/blog
5. Net entry: www.chetanbhagat.com/blog

One Night @the Call Center: How the Losers Can Turn It Around?

3

Chetan Bhagat's second novel, *One Night @ the Call Center* (2005), follows the black comedy genre that was well-established by him in his first work. Of course there are differences from the earlier work. The main actors are call centre operators—*losers* in the Metro hierarchy. These are the people who could not even make it to a prestigious educational institution. The jobs they hold are reasonably well-paid but absolutely soul-billing. They have to work all night to answer silly questions hurled by abusive and arrogant Americans. On top of that, they have to cope with a nasty boss, who is not only a fool but also a knave. All six major characters have a dark secret that keeps haunting them; their dreams are crushed, their ambitions thwarted. However, they keep on labouring, as the money is good and there is no choice either.

The novel begins rather dramatically. The author is travelling on a night train from Kanpur to Delhi, when a very pretty girl joins him in his coupe as a fellow-traveller. The author is simply enthralled by the long-tressed fairy (remember Keats and his *La Belle Dame Sans Merci*); there is a throbbing in his voice as he narrates that fateful meeting at night:

> But this night was different. Firstly, my compartment was empty. The railways had just started this new summer train and nobody knew about it. Secondly, I was unable to sleep.

I had come to IIT Kanpur for a talk. Before leaving, I drank four cups of coffee in the canteen chatting with the students. Bad idea, given it was going to be boring to spend eight insomniac hours in an empty compartment. I had no magazines or books to read. I could hardly see anything out of the window in the darkness. I prepared myself for a silent and dull night. Of course, it was anything but that.

She walked in five minutes after the train had left the station. She opened the curtains of my enclosure and looked puzzled.

'Is coach A4, seat 63 here?' she said.

The yellow lightbulb in my compartmet had a mood of its own. It flickered as I looked up to see her. 'Huh...' I said as I saw her face. It was difficult to withdraw from the gaze of her eyes.

'Actually it is. My seat is right in front of you,' she said and heaved her heavy suitcase on the upper berth. She sat down on the lower berth opposite to me, and gave out a sigh of relief.

'I climbed on the wrong coach. Luckily this train is connected,' she said, adjusting her long hair that ended in countless ringlets. From the corner of my eye I tried to see her. she was young, maybe early to mid twenties. Her waist length hair had a life of its own, a strand falling on her forehead repeatedly. I could not see her face closely, but I could tell one thing-she was pretty. And her eyes-once you looked into them, you could not turn away. I kept my gaze down.

She re-arranged stuff in her handbag. I tried to look out of the window. It was completely dark.

'So, pretty empty train,' she said after ten minutes.

'Yes, I said. It is the new holiday special. They just started it, without telling people about it.'

'No wonder. Otherwise, trains are always full at this time.'

> 'It will get full. Don't worry. Just give it a few days,' I said and leaned forward,' Hi, I am Chetan by the way, Chetan Bhagat.'
>
> 'Hi,' she said and looked at me for a few seconds, 'Chetan as in...I don't know, your name sounds familiar.'
>
> Now this was cool. It meant she had heard of my first book. I am recognized rarely, and of course, it had never happened with a girl on a night train.
>
> 'You might have heard of my book-*Five Point Someone*. I am the author,' I said.
>
> 'Oh yes,' she said and paused, 'Oh yes, of course. I have read your book. The three underperformers and the prof's daughter one, right?' she said.
>
> 'Yes,' I said, 'So how did you like it?'
>
> 'It was all right,' she said.
>
> I was taken aback. Man, I could have done with a little more of compliment here.
>
> 'Just all right?' I said, obviously fishing a bit too hard....[1]

The author is disappointed as he believes himself to be a youth icon—the voice of his generation. The unknown girl shocks him out of his comfort zone by telling him that he hardly knows the reality of the *losers,* who do not make it to the IIT. She tells

> 'At one level, you are hardly a youth writer.'
>
> I turned silent and looked at her for a few seconds. Her magnetic eyes had a soft but insistent gaze. 'I thought I wrote a book about college kids. That isn't youth?' I said.
>
> 'Yeah righ. So, you wrote a book on IIT. A place where so few people get to go. You think that represents the entire youth?' she said and took out a box of mints from her bag.
>
> She offered me one, but I declined. I wanted to get this straight.

> 'So what are you trying to say? I had to start somewhere, so I wrote about my college experiences. And you know the story is not so IIT specific. It could have happened anywhere. I mean, just for that you ore trashing my book.'
>
> 'I am not trashing it. I am just saying it hardly represents the Indian youth,' she said and closed back the box of mints.
>
> 'Oh really...,' I said but was interrupted by the noise as the train passed over a long river bridge. We didn't speak for the next three minutes, until the train returned to smoother tracks.
>
> 'What represents the youth?' I said.
>
> 'I don't know. You are the writer. You figure it out.' she said and brushed aside a few curls that had fallen on her forehead.
>
> 'That's not fair,' I said, 'that is so not fair,' I sounded like a five year old throwing a tantrum. She smiled as she saw me grumbling to myself. A few seconds later, she spoke again.
>
> 'Are you going to write more books?' she said.
>
> 'I'll try to,' I said. I wasn't sure if I ever wanted to talk to her again.
>
> 'So what is going to be? IIMs this time?' she said.
>
> 'No.'
>
> 'Why not?'
>
> (*ON@CC*, 4-5) (Emphasis added)

The fairy (*author's muse*) incites him further to look at the world around him, away from the ivory towers of IIT and IIM. What about some real Indian youth?, she asks. Consider her words:

> 'If you want to write about the youth, shouldn't you talk about young people who really face challenges? I mean yes, IITians face challenges, but what about the hundreds and thousands of other youth?'
>
> 'Like whom.'

> 'Just look around you. What is the biggest segment of youth facing challenges in modern India?'
>
> 'I don't know. Students?'
>
> 'Not those Mr. Writer. Get out of the student-campus of your first book now. Anything else you see that you find strange and interesting? I mean, what is the subject of your second novel?' she said. I turned up to look at her carefully for the first time. Maybe it was the time of the night, but I kid you not, she was one of the most beautiful women I had ever seen. Everything about her was perfect. Her face was like that of a child. She wore a little bindi, which was hard to focus on as her eyes came in the way.
>
> I went back to her question.
>
> 'Second novel? No, haven't thought of a subject yet,' I said.
>
> 'Really? Don't you have any ideas?'
>
> 'I do. But nothing I am sure about.'
>
> 'Interesting,' she drawled, 'Well, just bask in your first book then.'
>
> We kept quiet for the next half an hour. I took out the contents of my overnight bag and rearranged them for no particular reason. I wondered if it even made sense to change into a nightsuit. I was not going to fall asleep anyway. Another train noisily trundled past us in the opposite direction, leaving silence behind.
>
> 'I might have a story idea for you,' she said, almost startling me.
>
> (*ON@CC*, 5-6) (Emphasis added)

However, she has a pre-condition before she gives her story idea. The author has to promise that he will convert her story into a novel. He is reluctant to make a blind commitment but she is adamant:

> 'No. It is not about choice. If I tell you, you have to write it,' she said.
>
> 'Like write a whole book on it?' I said.

'Yes. Like it is your own story. In first person—just as your first book. I'll give you the contacts of people in the story. You can meet them, do your research, whatever it takes, but make it your second book.'

'Well then I think it is better if you don't tell me,' I said.

'Up to you,' she said and became quiet. She turned around to spread a bedsheet on her berth, and arranged the pillows and blankets. I guess she was planning to go to sleep.

I checked my watch again. It was 01:00 a.m. and I was still wide awake. This was a non-stop train, and there were no stations to look forward to until Delhi in the morning. She switched off the flickering yellow light. A mysterious blue light bulb was the only night light in the compartment. It felt strange, like we were the only two people in the universe.

As she was sliding under her blanket, I asked, 'What is the story about? At least tell me a little bit more.'

'Will you do it then?'

I shrugged in the semi-darkness. 'Can't say. Do not tell me the story yet. But at least tell me what it is about.'

She nodded and came out of her blanket. She sat cross-legged opposite me as she began talking.

'Alright,' she said, 'It is a story about six people in a call center on one night.'

'Just one night? Like this one?' I interrupted.

'Yes, one night. One night at the call center.'

'You sure that can be a full book? I mean, what is so special about this night?'

She heaved a sigh and took a sip from her bottle of mineral water.

'You see,' she said, 'It wasn't like any other night. It was a night there was a phone call'

'What?' I said and burst out laughing, 'So a call center gets a phone call. That is the special part?' She did not smile back. She waited for my amusement to end.

> 'You see,' she continued, 'It wasn't an ordinary phone call. It was the night... it was the night there was a phone call from God.'
>
> Her words had me spring to attention.
>
> 'What?'
>
> 'You heard me. That night there was a phone call from God,' she said.
>
> 'What exactly are you talking about?'
>
> 'I just told you what the story was about. You asked, remember?' she said.
>
> 'And then...how...I mean...'
>
> 'I am not telling you anymore. You know what the story is about. If you want to hear the story, you know my condition.'
>
> (*ON@CC*, 8-9) (Emphasis added)

The author is hooked, tempted by the phone-call from God. Still he demurs and the girl curls up to sleep. At last the author agrees to her condition and hears her story. He calls out to her:

> 'Listen,' I said, 'Get up. Sit down again.'
>
> 'Huh?' she said, rubbing her eyes, 'Why? What happened?'
>
> 'Nothing. You tell me what happened. Tell me the story,' I said.
>
> 'So you will write it?'
>
> 'Yes,' I said, with a bit of hesitation.
>
> 'Good,' she said, and sat up again. The cross-legged position was back.
>
> Over the rest of the night, she told me the story that begins from the next page. It is a story about six people, three guys and three girls who worked at the Connexions Call Center. I chose to tell the story through Shyam's eyes. This is because after I met him, I found him closest to me as a person. The rest of the

> people and what happened that night-well, I will let Shyam tell you that.
>
> (ON@CC, 10) (Emphasis added)

Shyam, obviously, is the *darker person* in each human being-the erotic, instinctive half of the human persona in *Jungian* terms. Carl Jung redefined the fractured human psyche as the coexistence in the human persona of the *White Consciousness* (rationality) and *Black Consciousness* (instinctive life). James Mersmann explains the Jungian vision:

> (instinctive life) threatens to break through as a shroudy stranger or shadow—There is in each of us an archetypal darker brother...associated with the body and the libido; the bright self...is associated with the head and rational faculties.[2]

By the end of the narrative Chetan Bhagat admits that *Shyam* is his alter-ego, his *darker-brother* faced with the problems he himself faced—a troublesome boss and love threatened by an NRI outsider.

> 'Shyam. Like I said, he and his story are a lot like mine. I relate to him a lot; I had similar problems. My own dark side.'
>
> 'Really? That's interesting,' she said. 'It is true though, we all have a dark side-something we don't like about ourselves, something that makes us angry and something we want to change about ourselves. The difference is how we choose to face it.'
>
> (ON@CC, 273) (Emphasis added)

Shyam, the narrator, is introduced to the readers first. He is the family black sheep, a call center worker in a family of professionals, and achievers. He is seen just leaving for work at Connexions Call Center in Gurgaon:

> I waved a goodbye to everyone, but no one acknowledged me. It wasn't surprising, I am only cared for so much. Every cousin of mine is becoming a doctor or engineer. You can say I am the black sheep of my family. Though I do not think that expression is correct. After all, what's wrong with black sheep—

> don't people wear black sweaters? But you get an idea of my status in my clan. In fact, the only reason people somewhat talk to me is I have a job and get a salary at the end of the month. You see, I used to work in the website department of an ad agency before this call center job.
>
> (*ON@CC*, 18)

The call center staff cab moves on to pick up the second member of the team, Radhika, who is a docile housewife having sacrificed her dreams to be a good teacher for the sake of an arranged marriage. She is lorded over by her mother-in-low and ignored by her husband. On top, the loser girl has to work all night at the call center. She is late that evening, as usual. She says to Shyam:

> 'Nothing. Almond milk for mom-in-law. Took longer to crush the almonds,' she said, leaning back exhausted in her seat. She had taken the middle seat.
>
> 'Ask mom-in-law to make her own milk,' I suggested.
>
> 'C'mon Shyam,' she said, 'she's so old, it is the least I can do, especially when her son is not here.'
>
> 'Yeah, right,' I shrugged. 'Just that and cooking three meals a day and household chores and working all night and...'
>
> 'Shh...' she said, 'forget all that. Any news on the call center? I'm scared.'
>
> (*ON@CC*, 20)

The next stop is to pick up Military Uncle, a retired army man who has been deserted by his son, who has settled down in the U.S.A. He has to work at the call center to supplement his meagre pension. He is a quiet, morose person who rarely speaks and looks after the email section. The next member of the team is Esha Singh, an aspiring model who has to earn her living while looking for a break. Later it is revealed that she has been a Casting-Couch victim-another loser.

She is glamorous and well-dressed as she appears:

> The driver drove to Esha Singh's (or agent Eliza Singer's) place next. She was already outside her house.

> The driver kept the Qualis ignition on as he opened the back door.
>
> Esha entered the Qualis and the smell of expensive perfume filled the vehicle, she sat next to Radhika in the middle row and removed her suede jacket.
>
> 'Mmm...nice. What is it?' Radhika said.
>
> 'You noticed...' Esha was pleased. 'Escape, by Calvin Klein.'
>
> (*ON@CC*, 21)

After Esha enters the real protagonist of the novel, Varun Malhotra, called Vroom by his friends as he is fond of wheels. He is angry and rebellious, though very bright and smart. He reminds the reader of Ryan in Five Point Someone. He is innovative, having designed a Troubleshooting website for the benefit of the call center users. His angst is rooted in the soured up relations between his parents, as he tells his co-workers:

> We had to pick Vroom next; his real, name is Varun Malhotra (or agent Victor Mell). However, everyone calls him Vroom because of his love for anything on wheels.
>
> The Qualis turned into the lane of Vroom's house. He was sitting on his bike, waiting for us.
>
> 'What's the bike for?' I said, craning out of the window.
>
> 'I'm coming on my own,' Vroom said, adjusting his leather gloves. He wore black jeans and trekking shoes that made his thin legs look extra long. His dark blue sweatshirt had the Ferrari horse logo on it.
>
> 'Are you crazy?' I said. 'It's so cold. Get in, we're late already.'
>
> Dragging the bike he came and stood next to me.
>
> 'No, I'm stressed today. I need to get it out of me with a fast ride.' He was standing right beside me and only I could hear him.
>
> 'What happened?'

> 'Nothing. Dad called. He argued with mom for two hours. Why did they separate? They can't live without screaming their guts out at each other?'
>
> (*ON@CC*, 23)

The last team-mate they pick up is Priyanka, Shyam's former girl-friend. Shyam still loves her, though he is sulking. To spite her, he has picked up another girl, Shefali, who is a real fool. As Priyanka joins them one notices Shyam's tantrums:

> 'Hi,' Priyanka said, as she entered the Qualis and sat next to Esha in the middle seat. She carried a large, white plastic bag apart from her usual giant handbag.
>
> 'Hi,' everyone replied except me.
>
> 'I said hi, Shyam,' Priyanka said.
>
> I pretended not to hear. It is strange, but ever since we broke up, I find it difficult to talk to her. Even though I must think of her thirty times a day.
>
> I looked at her, she adjusted her dupatta around her neck. The forest green salwar kameez she was wearing was new, I noticed. The colors suited her light brown skin. I looked at her nose and her nostrils that flared up every time she was upset. I swear tiny flames appeared in them when she was mad.
>
> 'Shyam, I said hi,' she said again. She gets really pissed if people don't respond to her.
>
> 'Hi,' I said. I wondered if Bakshi would finally promote me after he saw my website manual tonight.
>
> (*ON@CC*, 25-26) (Emphasis added)

Shyam thinks that with his promotion Priyanka's family may accept him as their son-in-law. However, it is later revealed that her parents have found an NRI match for her, a geek called Ganesh who works for *Microsoft*.

The last major player to enter the cast is Bakshi, the perverse call center boss, who puts on managerial airs and humiliates his subordinates, specially Shyam who is a quiet and simple boy. Shyam displays his personality in these words:

> His face shone as usual. It was the first thing you noticed about Bakshi—the oilfields on his face. I think

> if you could recreate Bakshi's skin as our landscape, you could solve India's oil problems. Priyanka told me once that when she met Bakshi for the first time, she had had an overwhelming urge to take a tissue and wipe it hard across his face. I do not think one tissue would be enough though.
>
> Bakshi was around thirty but looked forty and spoke like he was fifty. He had worked in Connexions for the past three years. Before that, he did an MBA from some unpronounceable university in South India. He thought he was Michael Porter or something (Porter is this big management guru, I didn't know either, but Bakshi told me in an FYl once) and loved to talk in manager's language or Managese, which is another language like English and American.
>
> 'So, how are the resources doing?' Bakshi said, swivelling on his chair. He never refers to us as people; we are all resources.
>
> (*ON@CC*, 52) (Emphasis added)

Under Bakshi's management, the call center is losing business and the jobs of all workers are at stake. At the same time the love-lifes of all the young players are in a tangle. Put in a nutshell the themes of *ON@CC* are love lost, thwarted ambitions, absence of family affection, pressures of a patriarchal set up, and the work environment of a globalized office. Shyam loves but has lost Priyanka, who is now planning an arranged marriage with another; Vroom loves Esha; Esha wants to be a model; Radhika is in an unhappy marriage with a demanding mother-in-law; and Military Uncle wants to talk to his grandson. They all hate Bakshi, their cruel boss. Claimed to be based on a true story, the novel relates to the lives of Indian youth trapped between new ambitions and old tradition.

The themes involve the anxieties and insecurities of the rising Indian middle class, including questions about career inadequacy, marriage, family conflicts in a changing India, and the relationship of the young Indian middle class to both executives and ordinary clients whom they serve in the U.S.A.

There is an aspect of self-help in the book as the author invites readers to identify aspects of themselves and their lives that make them angry and that they would like to change. One of the salient features of this novel is that all the characters experience a dramatic and disturbing event during the night when they receive a call from God, and all use this moment to re-examine their own lives.

Shyam is very upset to learn that Priyanka is engaged to a person called Ganesh Gupta, who works at Microsoft in the US. To add to his woes, he is horrified to learn that Bakshi has cheated him, and Vroom, by submitting the Troubleshooting Website to the Boston center as his own without crediting him and Vroom.

Priyanka is first happy when she is engaged to Ganesh Gupta, who works for Microsoft but becomes furious when she hears that her parents have planned her marriage the very next month, which she feels is too early. Both her mother and Ganesh press her to agree to this proposal. She is even more saddened by the fact that Shyam was eavesdropping on her conversation with Ganesh. When Vroom and Shyam show her that Ganesh had forged his pictures to hide his baldness, she disapproves Ganesh for having cheated her.

Esha had earlier done a compromise by sleeping with a designer to get a modelling contract. However the guy turned out to be opportunistic as he betrayed her by telling her she can't become a model due to her height. He also tried to console her by sending some money. Esha feels terribly betrayed and tries to suppress the mental pain by inflicting herself with physical pain by purposely cutting her skin.

Vroom is shocked to learn that Bakshi has cheated him and Shyam by submitting their work as his own. To add to his miseries, he overhears Esha telling the other girls that she had slept with a designer to get a modelling contract.

Radhika who loved her husband very much, is shocked to learn about his dark side. When Vroom calls up her husband pretending as a radio jockey and asks him to dedicate roses and a song to someone special, he chooses his girlfriend Payal over his wife. Radhika who listens to this gets terribly upset as her husband has betrayed her.

Military Uncle tries to be nice to his son and grandson. But when he sends some pictures via email to his grandson, his son loses his cool and asks him to keep out of his life. This leaves Military Uncle heartbroken.

The phone call from God is one of the salient features in the novel. The author has represented God a friendly figure rather than a boss. He is shown as speaking in modern English rather than the stereotypical pure English or Latin that one usually encounters God saying. The circumstances in which the characters of the novel get a phone call from God are the crisis points of their lives. In order to cheer themselves up they go to a night club. After enjoying for a while, they leave for office. Midway through the journey, Vroom starts to feel nauseated after drinking alcohol and so they stop and venture out. Vroom throws up and also breaks the window-pane of a shop thus spreading an alarm. They rush out of the place in fear. While returning, they face a life-threatening situation when their Qualis crashes into a construction site hanging over a mesh of iron construction rods. As the rods began to yield slowly, they started to panic. They are unable to call for help as there is no mobile phone network at that place. In this situation, Shyam's mobile phone starts ringing. The phone call is from God. He speaks to all of them and gives them suggestions to improve their life. After that, God also advises them on how to get the car back on the road. The interview with God moves them to the extent that they get ready to face their problems with utmost determination and motivation. Meanwhile Vroom and Shyam hatch up a plan to throw Bakshi out of the call center and prevent the closing of Conneions Call Center, whose employees are to be downsized radically. When they emerge out of danger, they have clear-cut goals in their mind. On returning to the call center, they carry out their plans with dexterity.

The phone-call from God is the climactic moment that changes the lives of each of these loser characters. God asks them to confess their mistakes and share their ambitions with him and he will rescue them from their death-trap. The whole scene is wonderfully conceived and scripted. The moment comes in chapter 30 as their Qualis hangs precariously over iron rods and scaffolding:

> ESHA'S FINGERS TREMBLED. SHE PRESSED THE BUTTON TO TAKE the call on speaker mode.
>
> 'Hi everyone. Sorry to call so late,' a cheerful voice came from the phone.
>
> 'Err. Who is it?' Esha said.
>
> 'It's God, the voice said.
>
> 'God? God as in...' Radhika said as all of us looked at the brightly-lit phone in fright.
>
> 'As in God. I noticed an unusual situation here, so I thought I would just check on you guys.'
>
> 'Who is this? Is this a joke?' Vroom asked in a stronger voice.
>
> 'Why? Am I being funny? I just said I am God,' the voice said.
>
> I narrowed my eyes. Apart from the fact that God using a cell phone was unusual, I never thought my life was important enough for God to call me.
>
> (*ON@CC*, 215) (Emphasis added)

God begins to question the trapped team about their status and priorities in life. All of them reply that their lives are in a mess, with no hope in sight. God's answer to their tales of woe is simple: they have to hear the voice of their conscience and choose the right path:

> 'The inner call.' God said.
>
> 'The inner call?' everyone said in unison.
>
> 'Yes, the little voice inside that wants to talk to you. But you can only hear it when you are at peace and then too it is hard to hear it. Because in modern life, the networks are too busy. The voice tells you what you really want. Do you know what I am talking about?'

(*ON@CC*, 117) (Emphasis added)

And finally God makes an offer. He will help them escape from death it they promise to do their Karma in accordance with their honest goals, and change their loser attitude to positive energy:

> 'Of course. Listen, I will make a deal with you. I will save your life tonight, but in return, you give me something. You close your eyes for three minutes. Think about what you really want and what you need to change in your life to get it. Then, once you get out of here, act on those changes. You do this and I will help you get out of this pit. Deal?'
>
> 'Deal,' I said.

(*ON@CC*) (Emphasis added)

Vroom's commitment is to quit the easy option and take up the challenge of fighting against social or political evil. He says:

> 'I want to have a life with meaning, even if it means a life without bed or daily trips to Pizza-Hut. I need to quit this call center. Sorry, but calling is not my calling, vroom said.

(*ON@CC*, 219)

Priyanka promises to defy her family and follow her instinctive love for Shyam and find a teaching job as well:

> 'I want my mother to be happy. But I cannot kill myself for it. My mother needs to realize a family is a great support to have, but ultimately, she is responsible for her own happiness. My focus should be on my own life and what I want,' Priyanka said.

(*ON@CC*, 219)

Military Uncle realizes how he has lost his son and his young family as he tried too much to control their lives. He will learn to adjust:

> 'I want to be with my son and my grandson. I miss them every moment. Two years ago, I used to live with them. But my daughter-in-law did things I didn't like—she

> went for parties, got a job when I wanted her to stay at home...I fought with them and moved out. But I was wrong. It is their life, and I have no right to judge them by my outdated values. And I need to get rid of my inflated ego and go to the US to see them and talk it out.'
>
> (*ON@CC*, 219)

Radhika wants to be rid of a dysfunctional marriage and her brutal mother-in-law:

> Radhika's turn came next. She fought back her tears as she spoke. 'I want be myself again, just like I was before marriage, when I was with my parents. I want to divorce Anuj. I don't want to ever look at my mother-in-law's face again. To do this, I have to accept that I made a wrong decision when I married Anuj.
>
> (*ON@CC*, 219-20)

Esha agrees to give up delusions of glamour and be realistic. She will not offer herself to be used again:

> Esha spoke after Radhika. 'I want my parents to love me again. I do not want to become a dumb model. I am sure I can find a better use for my looks, if they are worth anything. Any career that makes you compromise on our morals, or judges you because you are not an inch taller is not worth it.'
>
> (*ON@CC*, 220)

Shyam's commitment is the least complicated of all. He will chuck up this easy call center job and make a new start in life. He will find a backbone to stand up against those who have always used and abused him, thus being worthy of a girl like Priyanka:

> 'Okay. This will sound stupid, but I want to take a shot at my own business. I had this idea, if Vroom and I collaborate, we can set up a small web design company. That is all. But it may never work, because most of the things I do never work, but then...'
>
> 'And I want to be worthy of someone like Priyanka one day. I do not deserve her as of today, and I accept that...'

> 'Shyam, I never said...' Priyanka said.
>
> 'Please, let me finish Priyanka. It is about time people stop trampling all over me,' I said.
>
> (*ON@CC*, 220)

After hearing all these confessions and promises, God gives them four mantras of success. He tells the hopeless call center junkies:

> 'There are four things a person needs for success. I will tell you the two-obvious ones first. One, a medium amount of intelligence, and two, a bit of imagination. Agreed?'
>
> 'Agreed,' everyone said.
>
> 'And all of you have those qualities,' God said.
>
> 'What are the third and the fourth?' Vroom said.
>
> 'The third is what Shyam has lost,' God said.
>
> 'What's that?' I said.
>
> '**Self-confidence.** The third thing you need for success is self-confidence. But Shyam has lost it. He is hundred percent convinced he is good for nothing.'
>
> (*ON@CC*, 221) (Emphasis added)

The most interesting part of God's Sermon is the fourth dimension of success. It is Lord Krishna talking to Arjuna in *Sri Bhagvadgita*:

> 'The fourth ingredient is the most painful one. And it is something all of you still need to learn. Because it is often the most important thing,' God said.
>
> 'What?' I said.
>
> 'Failure,' God said.
>
> 'What? I thought you were talking about success,' Vroom said.
>
> 'Yes, but to be really successful, you must face failure. You have to experience it, feel it, taste it, suffer it. Only then can you shine,' God said...
>
> 'For, once you taste failure, you have no fear. You can take risks more easily. Then you don't want to snuggle

> in your comfort zone anymore—you are ready to fly. And success is about flying not snuggling God said.
>
> 'Point,' Priyanka said.
>
> 'So, here is a secret. Never be afraid of failure.'
>
> (*ON@CC*, 222-23) (Emphasis added)

The interview with God ends with a promise from Him as well:

> You do your best, and every now and then, I will come behind to give you a bonus push. But it has to begin with you. For otherwise I can't distinguish who needs my help most.'
>
> 'Point,' Vroom said.
>
> 'So, if I listen to my inner call and promise to do my best, will you be there for me?' I said.
>
> 'Absolutely.'
>
> (*ON@CC*, 224) (Emphasis added)

The words of God shall find much more relevance in Chetan Bhagat's third novel, *The 3 Mistakes of My Life*. But here too His exhortation inspires the trapped team to reverse the car, get away from death and find liberation from slavery at the call center. But before getting away, Vroom and Shyam get even with Bakshi for cheating and humiliating them. They save the call center jobs by telling the cowardly Americans that if they wish to survive they must remain connected to India. Finally Shyam and Priyanka rejoin in love while Vroom and Shyam become partners to float a web designing company. The novel ends with a *feel good* factor, as the closing remarks of Shyam testify:

> So looks like things are working out. As for me as a person, I still feel the same for the most part. However, there is a difference. I used to feel I was a good-for-nothing non-achiever. But that is not true. After all, I helped save lots of jobs at a call center, taught my boss a lesson, started my own company, was chosen over a big-catch NRI groom by a wonderful girl and now I even finished a whole book. This means that (i) I can

> do whatever I realy want (ii) God is always with me and (iii) there is no such thing as a loser after all.
>
> (*ON@CC*, 271) (Emphasis added)

ON@CC was a huge success, topping the popularity charts for months. It was also re-worked as a film entitled *Hello* that was a moderate hit. It is a fast-paced narrative as all events are focused on one night, though the flash-backs of Shyam-Priyanka love scenes pause the story for a while. It is a dark comedy which fuses the emotions of love and anger, hilarity and suffering, failure and success. It also makes a serious point that India is losing her freedom to American Coca-Colonization. India, the author feels, shall have to find her own identity if she has to be counted as a world-power.

Some reviewers have attacked ON@CC as a poor follow up novel to Five Point Someone. Their demolition job is based on two central points. First, they say, Chetan Bhagat has indulged in needless America-bashing and secondly God does not make phone calls. The first objection is partially valid as Bhagat seems to dismiss Americans as cowardly morons. But one must remember how vulnerable and fearful America looked after 9/11. And the Americans with their big-brother brashness often bully the developing nations to toe their line. However, as far as the God part is concerned, Chetan had foreseen such criticism and in the Epilogue he has offered an alternative scene for those who do not believe. It may not be God but Military Uncle talking to his juniors in their frightful condition. He advises them about the inner voice and courage of conviction. However, one should also consider what Chetan Bhagat's God is. He is not the God of theism but the voice of idealism (Purusha) that resides in every human heart. Paul Tillich, in his brilliant work on existential philosophy, has called this power God above all Gods. He writes in his seminal treatise, *The Courage to Be*:

> And one can become aware of the God above the God of theism in the anxiety of guilt and condemnation when the traditional symbols that enabled men to withstand the anxiety of guilt and condemnation have lost their power. When divine judgement is interpreted

> as a psychological complex and forgiveness as a remnant of the father-image, what once was the power in those symbols can still be present and create the courage to be in spite of the experience of an infinite gap between what we are and what we ought to be. The lutheran courage returns but not supported by the faith in a judging and forgiving God. It returns in terms of the absolute faith which says Yes although there is no special power that conquers guilt. The courage to take the anxiety of meaninglessness upon oneself is the boundary line up to which the courage to be can go. Beyond it is more non-being. Within it all forms of courage are re-established in the power of the God above the God of theism. The courage to be is rooted in the God who appears when God has disappeared in the anxiety of doubt.[3]

Chetan Bhagat's weltanschuuang exhorts his readers to discover such a God above all gods, the God that moves man to determined participation in life, the God that opens up a possibility of human good, the God who is invoked in the philosophy of *Bhagvadagita*:

11:28 क्लैव्यं मा स्म गमः पार्थ नैतत्वरूयुपद्यते।
श्रुदं हृदयदौर्बल्यं स्वक्वोत्ति ठ परात।।

(Yield not to impotence, O Parttha (O son of Pritha). It does not befit thee. Cast off this mean weakness of heart stand up, O parantapa.)

11:38 सुखदुःख समे कत्वा लाभलाभौ जयाजयौ।
ततो युद्दयस्व नैवं पापभ्वाप्स्यसि।

(Having made pleasure and pain, gain and loss, victory and defeat the same, engage thou in battle for the sake of battle; thus thou shalt not incur sin.)

With such determination, says Lord Krishna, one should plunge into the battle of life; and such a participant shall be free from all doubts and anxieties, because he is aware of a God above souls, who resides in his soul:

VI:29 सर्वभूतस्थमात्मानं सर्वभूतानि चात्मनि।
ईत्ततेयोगयुक्तात्मका सर्वत्रसमदर्शनः।।

(With the mind harmonised by Yoga he sees the Self, abiding in all beings and all beings in the Self; he sees the same everywhere.)

VI:30 यो मां पयाति सर्वत्र सर्व च मयि पयति।
तस्याह न प्रणयामिस च मे न प्रणायति।।

(He who sees me everywhere, and sees everything in Me, he never becomes separated from Me, nor do I become separated from him.)

VI:31 सर्वभूतस्थितं यो मां भजत्येकत्वमास्थितः।
सर्वथा वर्तमानो पि स योगी मयि वर्तते।

(He who being established in unity, worships Me who dwells in all beings, that Yogi abides in Me, whatever his mode of living maybe.[4])

As Bhagat's *ON@CC* ends, his central characters have also attained this equanimity-Santih- of the greatest Yogi who rises above the pain of personal sorrow towards the joy of human brotherhood. They are dedicated to the values of niskama karma, where human and divine entities are fused into a great soul, where man discovers God above all gods.

Notes

1. Chetan Bhagat: *One Night @ the Call Center* (Delhi, Rupa, 2005) pp. 1-3) (Emphasis added) (All subsequent citations are from this edition and the page no's have been given in parenthesis)
2. James Mersmann: 'Allen Ginsberg' in *American Writes(ed.)* A.W. Litz, Supp. ll Vol. I (New York, Scribners, 1981) p. 312
3. Paul Tillich: *The Courage to Be* (New Haven, Yale Univ. Press, 1952), pp. 182-90 (Emphasis added)
4. A.C. Bhaktivedanta: *Bhagvadgita-As It Is* (Mumbai, Bhaktivedanta Book Trust, 2010), pp. 101-110

The 3 Mistakes of My Life: The Underbelly of Indian Metro Society

Chetan Bhagat's third novel, ironically titled *The 3 Mistakes of My Life* (2008), goes down a notch in social hierarchy to explore the lives and passions of youth in an emerging Metro. The locale is Ahmedabad, the seat of Chetan's second alma mater, Indian Institute of Management. However, the IIM is not the focus of narration at all, rather it is the down market area of the old city where the story takes place. The three strands that intertwine to make the fable are the three passions of contemporary Indian youth—career ambitions, religious identity and cricket. The three friends who play the protagonists in the story are Govind Patel (also the narrative voice), the son of a widow who is good at studies, specially Maths; Ishaan, the son of a telephone department employee, who is a deserted NDA cadet and a good but frustrated cricketer; and Omi, the son of a priest of Swamibhakti temple. The scene is downtown Ahmedabad, a growing city still trapped in the prejudices of old India:

> Yes, Ahmedabad is my city. It is strange, but if you have had happy times in a city for a long time, you consider it the best city in the world. I feel the same about Ahmedabad. I know it is not one of those hip cities like Delhi, Bombay or Bangalore. I know people in these cities think of Ahmedabad as a small town, though that is not really the case. Ahmedabad is the

> sixth largest city in India, with a population of over five million. But I guess if you have to emphasise the importance of something, then it probably isn't as important in the first place. I could tell you that Ahmedabad has better multiplexes than Delhi or nicer roads than Bombay or better restaurants than Bangalore—but you will not believe me. Or even if you do, won't give a damn. I know Belrampur is not Bandra, but why should I defend being called a small-town-person as if it is a bad thing? A funny thing about small towns is that people say it is the real India. I guess they do acknowledge that at one level the India of the big cities is fake. Yes, I am from the old city of Amdavad and proud of it. We don't have as many fashion shows and we still like our women to wear clothes. I don't see anything wrong with that.[1]

The passions of the three friends are clearly defined at the very outset:

> I wasn't sure if Omi really believed in what he said, or if he was revising lessons given by Parekh-ji. He never spoke about this to Ish and me, but, somewhere deep down, did he also feel like Bittoo Mama? If Ish's passion was cricket and my passion was business, was omi's passion religion? Or maybe, like most people, he was confused and trying to find his passion. And unlike us who never took him seriously, perhaps Parekh-Ji gave him a sense of purpose and importance. (*3 Mistakes,* 69) (Emphasis added)

The story, however, begins at the end, before the events are narrated by Govind Patel to the author. Chetan Bhagat gets an email in Singapur from a youth, who signs as G P, that he is committing suicide with an overdose of sleeping pills. The worried author calls up his old professor at the IIM to locate the unfortunate boy at any city hospital. The professor obliges by finding one Govind Patel and Chetan rushes to meet him in Ahmedabad. Initially the youngman refuses to talk to him. However, after much cajoling and coercion he narrates to the author his sad experiences that have led to the suicide attempt.

He begins with talking of his two friends, Ishaan the angry rebel, who is extra-protective of his young sister, Vidya, and a huge cricket enthusiast; and Omi, the simpleton who blindly follows Hindu rites, being a priest's son. They are two losers, poor in studies and rejected as no-gooders. Govind is a bright student who gives tuitions in Maths to school students and hopes to become a big business tycoon one day. He is a true blood Gujarati who hopes to make it big one day. He represents the ethos of his soil:

> There is something about Gujaratis, we love business. Amdavadis love it more than anything else. Gujarat is the state in India where people tend to respect you more if you have business than if you are in service. The rest of the country dreams about a cushy job that gives a steady salary and provides stability. In Ahmedabad, service is for the weak. That was why I dreamt the biggest dream—to be a big businessman one day. The only problem was my lack of capital. But I would build it slowly and make my dream come true. Sure; Ish could not make his dream of being in the Indian cricket team real, but that was a stupid dream to begin with. To be in the top eleven of a country of a billion people was in many ways an impossible dream, and even though Ish was top class in Belrampur, he was no Tendulkar. My dream was more realistic. I would start slow and then grow my business. From a turnover of thousands, to lakhs, to crores and then to hundreds of crores. (3 *Mistakes,* 12)

However, his big ambitions led to what he calls *the first mistake of his life.* He challenges the Hindu ethos of acceptance by making attempts to rise beyond the destined station of life. He recalls after a huge loss caused by the Bhuj earthquake of January, 2001:

> India is not a place for dreams. Especially when you have failed once. I finally saw the sense inherent in the Hindu philosophy of being satisfied with what one had, rather than yearn for more, it wasn't some cool philosophy that ancient sages invented, but a survival

> mantra in a country where desires are routinely crushed. This shop in the temple was my destiny, and earning that meagre income from it my karma. More was not meant to be. I breathed out, felt better and opened the cash drawer.
>
> (*3Mistakes,* 115) (Emphasis added)

Govind, Ish and Omi begin a small sports goods business in the temple courtyard; the little shop being available because of Omi's family. 'Team India Cricket Shop' opens for business in April 2000. Ish being a cricketer is a big help as he offers his services free to coach youngsters about how to bat or bowl. Business slowly grows and they add another service—paints, notebooks, pencils and other school items. Govind keeps account carefully, and books a new business premises at an upcoming mall at Navrangpura on the outskirts of Ahmedabad. He hopes to move to a swanky store far from the dingy temple stall. However, his hopes are dashed by the earthquake:

> Two years of scrimping and saving, twenty years of dreams—all wiped away in twenty seconds. The Navrangpura Malli's neon sign, once placed at the top of the six floor building, now licked the ground. Maybe this was God's way of saying something—that we shouldn't have these malls. We were destined to remain a small town and we shouldn't even try to be like the big cities. I don't know why I thought of God, I was agnostic. But who else do you blame earthquakes on?
>
> Of course, I could blame the builder of the Navrangpura's mall. For the hundred-year-old buildings in the old city pols remained standing. Omi's two-hundred-year-old temple stood intact. Then why did my fucking mall collapse? What did he make it with? Sand?
>
> I needed someone to blame. I needed to hit someones, something. I lifted a brick, and threw it at on already smashed window. The remaining glass broke into little bits. (*3 Mistakes,* 108)

The hammer of God unnerves Govind; he groans in the pain of dead dreams. He was an agnostic and thus ready to blame God or nature for such cruel acts that destroy human life:

> We lost everything. Look, our business collapsed even before it opened....
>
> I broke down. I never cried the day my father left us. I never cried when my hand had got burnt one Diwali and Dr. Verma had to give me sedatives to go to sleep. I never cried when India lost a match. I never cried when I couldn't join engineering college. I never cried when we barely made any money for the first three months of business. But that day, when God slapped my city for no reason, I cried and cried. Ish held me and let me use his shirt to absorb my tears.
>
> 'Govi, let's go home,' Ish said. He never shortened my name before. He'd never seen me like that too. Their CEO and parent had broken down.
>
> (3 *Mistakes*, 109)

Ish and Omi console him and ask him to go back to the temple shop and try all over again. In his depression he goes to a doctor who advises him to keep his hopes alive as he is a Gujarati:

> 'I didn't expect this from you. You have heard of Navaldharis.' Dr. Verma Said.
>
> I kept quiet.
>
> 'You can talk. I haven't put a thermometer in your mouth.'
>
> 'No, who are they?'
>
> 'Navaldharis is a hardcore entrepreneur community in Gujarat. Everyone there does business. And they say, a true Navaldhari businessman is one who can rise after being razed to the ground nine times.'
>
> 'I am in debt, Doctor. I lost more money in one stroke than my business ever earned...

> 'I don't feel like doing anything. This earthquake, why did this happen? Do you know our school, is now a refugee camp?' (*3 Mistakes,* 110-111)

He takes this sane advice and starts again. This time he works out a new business model—supplying sports goods to schools and colleges. His plan works and business booms. Luckily for the boys, Indian cricket team starts winning against formidable rivals like Australia, and more youngsters take to the game:

> Business exploded in the next three months. Every Indian kid played cricket in May and June. Experts had called the India-Australia series historic. The actual matches had taken place during the exams. The pent-up cricket fix came out properly only in the vocations.
>
> (*3 Mistakes,* 148)

The first mistake is partly rectified and life comes back on track for the three youngsters.

However, more trouble is in store for Govind though it comes as a blessing. He starts giving Maths tuitions to Ishaan's younger sister, Vidya, who is something of a beauty as well as a flirt. Her parents wish her to join a medical college, though she wants to be a fashion designer. Govind moves fast from being a teacher to a friend as they visit book-shops and share ice-creams. Vidya is not keen in Maths, and tempts him to come closer:

> 'Be serious, Vidya. This is not right. I am your teacher, your brother trusts me as a friend, I have responsibilities—loans, business and a mother. You are not even eighteen.'
>
> 'Two months,' she wiggled two fingers. 'Two months and I will turn eighteen. Time to bring me another nice gift. Anyway, please continue.'
>
> 'Well, whatever. The point is, significant reasons exist for me not to indulge in illogical emotions. And I want...'
>
> She stood up and came to my side. She sat on the flimsy armrest of my plastic chair.

> She put her finger on my mouth. She cupped my face in her palms.
>
> 'You don't shave that often eh? Ew,' she said. She threw a tiny spit ball in the air.
>
> 'What?' I said and looked at her.
>
> 'I think a mosquito kissed me,' she said and spit again, 'is it still there in my mouth?'
>
> She opened her mouth and brought it close. Her lips were eight millimetres apart from mine.
>
> Soon the gap reduced to zero. I don't know if I came towards her or she came towards me.
>
> (*3 Mistakes*, 183)

Blinded by young love and rising sexual passion, Govind commits what he calls the second mistake of his life: he has sexual relations with his best friends sister. The occasion is Vidya's birthday and the two friends go up to the terrace to celebrate with coffee and cake. The small cassette-plyer rings with the rebellious music of Boyzone when Govind and Vidya move closer:

> She released my hand as I sat down again. She looked beautiful as the candlelight flickered on her face. A song called 'No matter what' started to play. Like with all romantic songs, the lyrics seemed tailor-made for us.
>
> *No matter what they tell us*
> *No matter what they do*
> *No matter what they teach us*
> *What we believe is true*
>
> She kissed me like she never had before. It wasn't like she did anything different, but there seemed to be more feeling behind it. Her hands came to my shoulders and under my shirt. The music continued.
>
> *I can't deny what I believe*
> *I can't be what I'm not*
> *I know this love's forever*
> *That's all that matters now*

> I don't know if it was the candlelight or the birthday mood or the cushions or what. But it was then that I made **the second mistake** of my Life.
>
> I opened the top button of her kurti and slid my fingers inside. A voice inside stopped me, I took my hand out. But she continued to kiss me as she unbuttoned the rest of her top. She pulled my fingers there again.
>
> 'Vidya...' By this time my hand was in places impossible to withdraw from for any guy. So, I went with the flow, feelings, desire, nature or whatever else people called the stuff that evaporated human rationality.
>
> She took off her kurti. 'Remove your hand, they won't run away.'
>
> 'Huh?' I said.
>
> 'How else do I remove this?' she said, pointing to her bra. I moved my hands to her stomach as she took the bra off and lay on top of me.
>
> 'Take if off,' she said, tugging at my shirt. At this point, I could have jumped off the terrace if she asked me to. I followed her instruction instantly.
>
> (*3 Mistakes*, 199-200) (Emphasis added)

The second mistake is not far away. Vidya puts Govind's hand on her breast and all sense slips away as emotions rush:

> The music didn't stop, and neither did we. We went further and further as the tiny candles burned out one by one. Sweat beads glistened on your bodies. Vidya didn't say anything throughout, part from one time in the middle.
>
> 'Arc you going to go down on me?' she said, after she had done the same to me.
>
> I went down, and came back up. We looked into each other's eyes as we became one. The screams from the pols continued as England lost wickets.
>
> Only four candles remained burning by the time we finished. We combined the six cushsions to make one

> mattress and lay on it. Only after we were done did we realise how cold and chilly it really was. We covered ourselves in my jacket and dug our cold feet inside the lower cushions.
>
> 'Wow, I am an adult and am no longer a virgin, so cool. Thank God,' she said and giggled. She cuddled next to me. A sense of reality struck as the passion subsided. What have you done Mr. Govind Patel?
>
> (*3 Mistakes*, 201)

Later in the story Ishaan comes to know about this sexual relationship and breaks off with Govind. This mistake takes a longer time to rectify. It is only after the suicide attempt that Ish relents and visits the hospital with Vidya:

> Govind's eyelashes flickered and everyone moved closer to the bed.
>
> 'Ish? Vidya!' Govind blinked.
>
> 'There are better ways to attract attention,' Vidya said.
>
> 'When did you come?' Govind asked, quite forgetting the others.
>
> 'I left my marketing class halfway,' Vidya said. 'But that doesn't mean I forgive you for not replying to me. Or for popping these pills. I never popped anything even when I was most scared, you know when.'
>
> 'Your parents told you not to speak to me again.
>
> Ish wanted the same.'
>
> 'So?' Vidya removed her college bag from her shoulder and placed it on the bed. 'What did your heart want?'
>
> (*3 Mistakes*, 255)

The thread of relations is joined again and Govind is accepted by Vidya's family. She is last seen visiting him with a bouquet in hand. The author reports:

> I met Vidya at the hospital entrance as I left. She was wearing a green Lehanga, probably her most cheerful dress, to lift Govind's spirits. She carried a bouquet.
>
> 'Nice roses,' I said.

> 'Law Garden has the best ones. I miss Ahmedabad, can't wait for my course to be over in six months,' she said.
>
> 'I thought you were a Bombay girl, trapped in the small city or whatever.'
>
> 'He told you everything? Like everything?' she, looked shocked.
>
> 'Pretty much.'
>
> 'Oh well, Bombay is nice, but my own is my own. *Pao bhaji* tastes much better in Ahmedabad.'
>
> I wanted to chat with her more, but had to leave. They had let me into their world, but I couldn't overstay.
>
> (*3 Mistakes*, 257)

The third mistake is more complicated and interwoven with the Post-Godhara communal riots in Ahmedabad. Omi's 'mama', Bittoo, is a Hindu activist and works for a right-wing political party. The three friends are more secular-minded and tolerant of Muslims. Ishaan takes a young cricket prodigy, Ali, under his wing and hopes to make him a national icon like Sachin Tendulkar. He coaches him and even arranges a scholarship for him to train at Australian Cricket Academy. Ali refuses to stay on in Australia and comes back home to India. But things go horribly wrong as Godhara happens. A train bogey full of Kar-Sevaks is burnt by Muslim hooligans and Bittoo Mama vows revenge, as his young son Dheeraj, was among the killed youth. His words are chilling:

> 'But the bastards made a big mistake. They tried to rape Gujarat today. 'Mother fuckers' thought these vegetarian people, what will they do? Come let's show them what we can do.'
>
> Mama paused to take a sip from his hips flask. We stepped back towards the bank.
>
> 'I hope they won't expect us to join. I won't,' I whispered in Ish's ear.

> 'Nor am I, and let's take Omi inside too,' Ish said. We told Omi to hide behind us. In a delicate movement, Ish shut the bank gate again and locked it.
>
> 'What are you whispering?' Mama said and almost lost his balance. His fire torch fell on the floor. The mob cleared around it. He lifted the torch back.
>
> 'Where is my other son? Open this gate,' Mama said as he couldn't see Omi.
>
> 'What do you want Mama? Can we talk tomorrow?' I said.
>
> 'No tomorrow, I want something today.'
>
> 'Mama, you know Omi needs to get home...,' I said. Mama brushed me away.
>
> 'I don't want Omi. I don't want any of you. I have many people to help me kill the bastards.'
>
> Ish came next to me. He held my hand tight.
>
> 'So leave us Mama,' Ish said.
>
> 'I want the boy. I want that Muslim boy,' Mama said.
>
> 'What?' Ish said.
>
> 'Eye for an eye. I'll slaughter him right here. Then I will cry for my son. Get the fucking boy,' Mama said and thumped Ish's chest. Ish struggled to stand straight. (*3 Mistakes,* 223)

All hell breaks loose on the streets of Ahmedabad. Ishaan locks Ali up in an abandoned bank vault and fights to save him from Hindu mobs. Bittoo Mama surrounds the bank with his crazy, angry followers and a bitter struggle follows:

> My hands shivered as I tackled another fat man. My wicket got stuck in his trishul's blades. Our conjoined weapons hurled in the air as we tried to extract them apart. He kicked me in my right knee and I lost my balance. He came forward and pinned me to the wall.
>
> The third man hit Ish on the neck with the blunt end of the trishul. Ish fell forward. The man took Ish captive and pushed him against the wall.

> Omi had crushed the toes of the fourth man with the bat. The man winced as he fell on the floor. Omi kicked his stomach but the fifth man punched hard on Omi's back. The man grabbled Omi from behind.
>
> 'Buffalo, you can't get free now,' the man said.
>
> 'Tch, tch. Stupid bastards. Like playing with fire eh?' Mama said as he sat on the branch manager's table. The three of us were pinned to the wall. The three remaining able men had blocked our bodies with their trishuls.
>
> Mama sat on the branch manager's table and looked at us.
>
> 'I want blood. Give me the boy, or it will be yours,' Mama said. He took out his hip flask and had a big sip of whisky.
>
> 'There is no boy here,' Ish said, 'as you can see.'
>
> 'You are not to be trusted, as I have seen,' Mama said. He threw the empty flask at Ish. It hit him in the chest.
>
> Two injured men lay on the floor. Mama kicked them.
>
> 'Go search,' Mama said.
>
> The men hobbled and left the room.
>
> 'Nobody here,' they screamed as they traversed the various rooms of the bank. Their voice had pain. Something told me they'd had enough.
>
> (*3 Mistakes*, 239)

But Bittoo Mama does not give up. He follows the boys inside and demands Ali's head.

> Mama followed the sound. The sound came from the manager's table. Mama went to the wall behind the manager's table. It had the vault. The sound came from within the vault.
>
> 'Open this,' Mama said as he pointed to the wheel shaped lock of the vault.
>
> We kept quiet. Ish's phone rang again. I guessed Vidya had called to explain things to her brother.
>
> 'I said open this,' Mama said.

> 'This is the bank's vault. We don't have the keys,' I said. I wanted to do my part, to help Ish. I wanted to do anything to make me less of a creep.
>
> (*3 Mistakes*, 240)

However, Bittoo Mama is too angry to be controlled by reason:

> Mama came to Ish. He jabbed the blunt end of the trishul again at his chest wound.
>
> Ish screamed in pain and fell. The man searching Ish slapped him a few times. Ish clenched his teeth and continued to kick. Mama reached into Ish's pockets. He felt something. Ish had worn practice shorts underneath his pants. Mama took his hands out of the pants and slid it again into Ish's shorts. He pulled out a bangle sized keyring. It had two six inch long keys.
>
> Ish lay on the floor taking heavy breaths from his mouth. His eyes looked defiant even as his body refused to cooperate.
>
> Mama twirled the key ring in his hand.
>
> 'Never looted a bank before,' Mama said, 'and what a prize today. Father and son, I'll root out the clan.'
>
> Mama took a minute to figure out the vault keys.
>
> 'Don't Mama, he is a child. For my sake,' Omi said.
>
> Mama paused and turned to look at us.
>
> 'My Dhiraj was also a child,' Mama said and went to the vault.
>
> (*3 Mistakes*, 240-41) (Emphasis added)

In the tragic aftermath both Omi and Bittoo Mama are dead, but Ali escapes, though badly injured. Govind feels that his cowardice was the cause of Ali's injury and blames himself:

> Mama ran towards Ali. I knew I had to get out of the captor's grip, grab Ali and pull him to my side. I got ready to move. However, I looked at Mama. The sight of his huge frame and a sharp weapon sent a fear inside me. And I wasted precious time thinking when I should have acted. Ish and I exchanged another glance and he saw my fear mixed with self-interest. What if

> the trishul ends in my stomach? The what-ifs made me hesitant, but I snapped myself out of it and made a dive to my left. I grabbed Ali and pulled him towards me. Mama struck, but missed Ali's torso. One blade of the trishul jabbed Ali's wrist. Ali would have been completely unhurt only if I had dived a second earlier. And here it was, something I didn't realise then, the one second delay being the third big mistake of my life.
>
> Of course, I didn't know I had made a mistake then.
>
> Ish did exactly as I thought, and banged his head against the captor's to set himself free. It would have hurt Ish, but I think Ish was beyond pain right now. Ish took his captor's trishul and struck it into the man's heart. The man screamed once and turned silent.
>
> Ish ran to us.
>
> 'He's ok, he is ok,' I said turning to Ish. I held Ali tight within me in an embryo position.
>
> (*3 Mistakes*, 246) (Emphasis added)

This mistake is also rectified ultimately. Ali undergoes an operation in London and Govind pays for the treatment. As Govind recovers from his suicide-attempt he gets the news of Ali's recovery and he sends an SMS to the author:

> The next morning I woke up early. I had an SMS from Govind.
>
> doc approves ali 2 play.
> fingers X. pls pray.
> fingers X. pls. pray.
> v hit pitch 2mrow.
>
> I went to office the next day. London is eight hours behind Singapore, and I checked my phone during my evening coffee at 4 p.m. I had no message. I left office at 8 p.m. I was in the taxi when my phone beeped.
>
> ish bowls 2 ali,
> ali moves fwd & turns.
> straight 6...!

Thus ends the fable of 3 mistakes. Things go horribly wrong and then come back on track. Life is long equation which cannot be fully and finally solved. What one can do is to make the best use of it, as Govind tells Vidya:

> 'Figuring out the maths of life is more important,' I said. 'What's that?'
>
> 'Who you are, what do you want versus what people expect of you. And how to keep what you want without pissing off people too much. Life is an optimisation problem, with tons of variables and constraints.
>
> (*3 Mistakes,* 198) (Emphasis added)

The novel's message is that victory and defeat are parts of human life and we should never think of suicide. Ups are followed by downs but life never ends. What Chetan Bhagat wishes to convey to Indian youth can be understood with reference to a brief article published in *The Times of India.* Swami Sukhodhanand writes:

> It is better to play to win than to lose; it is better to wear out than to rust out. It is better to aim for excellence and not get lost in success. When one puts oneself on the track of excellence, it brings out inherent talents to light. It is said those who have never angered anyone is a failure in life. Similarly, a person who has never lost has never found the joy of winning.
>
> No doubt there is a joy in winning and pain in losing and if one does not accept both then it is like expecting the river to have one bank, the river is contained by two sides of the bank, is it not?
>
> Winning involves four important dimensions: Self-confidence, mental toughness, winning-oriented thinking and the ability to be innovative. Self-confidence stands on three important pillars: feeling good, taking responsibility and developing skills. One has to learn the art of feeling good even in moments of pressure.
>
> The quality of life is the quality of one's consistent emotion. One has to master the art of keeping emotion

> in a state of well being; search for such a state of consciousness. At moments of pressure, the mind tends to validate itself unconsciously on incidents where one is in pressure.
>
> In cricket when wickets are falling, new players are under great pressure. Past failures will influence present situations. So we are not living in the present but we are living in our past. In my interactions with cricket players I tell them that when they are under pressure, they should consciously recreate their future and not their past. How can one do that? That is the responsibility and discipline one should have.[2]

Quite like Swamiji, Chatan Bhagat has used, in *3 Mistakes*, cricket as a metaphor of life. Just as in sport, life is an unending sequence of rises and falls, ups and downs. The important thing is the constant flow of the game; the show must go on. As in cricket, life affords a second innings when things lost may be regained; what is broken may be repaired; the story may be turned over its head. This is exactly what happins in the Second Test Match of the India-Australia series of 2001; a humdinger of a contest staged at India's biggest cricket ground, the Eden Gardens in Kolkata. Let the story be told in excerpts chosen from the novel:

> Day 1
>
> Most of the time crap happens in life. However, sometimes miracles do too. To us, the second test match of the India-Australia series was the magic cure for the quake. I remember everyday of that match. Ish continued with his weird and highly improbable ideas of making Ali meet the Australian team.
>
> 'They are raping us again. Fuck, business is never going to pick up,' I said as I saw the score. On the first day at tea, Australia's score was 193/1.
>
> 'If it does. I said if,' Ish said, upset at the score more than me.
>
> I looked at the TV. Perhaps God listened to Mrs. Ganguly's prayers inside. A little known Surd called

Harbhajan Singh had bowled after tea. Wickets crumbled and from 193/1, Australia ended the day at 291/8.

Day 2

The only way to describe the second day of the match was depressing. From 291/8, Australia dragged on their first innings to end at a healthy 445 all out. The Indians came out to bat and opener Ramesh got out for no score.

'Who the fuck is this Ramesh?' Connection quota,

Ish said.

But it wasn't only Ramesh who sucked. Tendulkar scored ten, others evenless. Dravid scored the highest at twenty-five. The second day ended with India at 128/8.

Ish tore his chapattis with anger over dinner. 'These Australians must be thinking-why even bother to come and play with India.'

Day 3

The next morning I don't know why we even bothered to switch on the TV. India struggled to stretch their first innings, but packed up before Lunch at 171 all out. 'And the Australians have asked India to follow on,' the commentator said and I slapped my forehead. A defeat on a test match was one thing, but an innings defeat meant empty parks for weeks. Kids would rather read textbooks than play cricket and be reminded of India's humiliation. Why on earth had I started this business? What an idiot I am? Why couldn't I open a sweet shop instead? Indians would always eat sweets. Why sports? Why cricket?...

Day 4

If there was a day that India dominated world cricket, it was on the fourth day of the match. Yes, India won the World Cup on 25 June 1983 and so that counted, too. But the day I'm talking about was when two

Indian batsmen made eleven Australian cricketers dance to their tune. They did it in public and they did it the whole day. That's right. On the fourth day of the Test, Ish didn't leave the TV. Even to pee.

Here is what happened. Laxman and Dravid continued to play and added 357 runs for the fifth wicket. Day 4 started at 274/4 and ended at 589/4. Nine of the eleven members of the Australian team took turns bowling, but none of them succeeded in getting a wicket. The crowd at Eden Gardens became possessed. They chanted Laxman's name enough times to make Steve Waugh visibly grumpy. The team that had given us a follow-on could not bowl one batsman out.

Day 5

Human expectations have no limit. While we were praying only for a draw two days ago, the start of the fifth day raised new hopes. Laxman left at 281 and everyone in the stadium stood up to applaud for his eleven-hour innings.

The Indian captain Ganguly made a surprise decision. After an hour's play for the day, he declared the Indian innings at 657/7. It meant Australia would have to come back and bat. And that they had to make 384 runs in the rest of the day to win the match.

Day 5-Post-tea

The Indian team must have mixed something special in their tea. Australia came back and continued to cruise at 166/3. Then came five deadly overs that included a hat-trick from Harbhajan Singh. Next stop, Australia 174/8. In eight runs, half of the Australian team was gone.

'Ish, don't fucking stand in front of the TV,' I said. But Ish wasn't standing, only jumping.

'Fuck your statistics man, fuck the probability,' Ish shouted in jubilation. I don't like it when people insult mathematics, but I gave Ish the benefit of doubt. You

> are allowed a few celebratory curses when you witness history.
>
> Pretty soon, the last two batsman were scalped as well. Harbhajan, the Surd that Ish kissed on screen (and left saliva marks all over), took six wickets, and India won the match in the most spectacular way ever.
>
> At Eden Gardens, every placard, every poster and anything combustible, besides people, was on fire. It was impossible to hear the TV commentary, as the crowds roared everytime an Indian team member's name was announced.
>
> Ish stood tall, his hands on his hips and looked at the screen. I could see genuine love in his eyes. Every now and then, I had seen Ish watch the men in blue as if he wished he was one of them. But today, he didn't have any of his own regrets. I think more than wanting to be them, he wanted them to win. He saw Harbhajan jump and jumped along. He clapped when Ganguly came to accept the trophy.
>
> (*3Mistakes,* 120-129) (Emphasis added)

Like the fortunes of the Indian team, the business of Govind and his friends rises, *Phoenix-like,* from the ashes. Their second innings goes on very well before *Godhara* happens and everything collapses again.

There is another aspect of cricket, specially for a pluralistic society like India. Economics and politics are divisive forces, but cricket is the big adhesive that cements Indian society in the game of cricket, there is no division of caste and creed. Consider the *World Cup* winning team of 2011. Led by a *Kumaoni* boy from Jharkand the team had *Hindu* players from the North, *Muslim* boys from Gujarat as well as *Sardars* from Punjab; and the coach was a *Christian* from South Africa. *But on the fateful day they were all Indians—no other identity was even mentioned.*

This is exactly the way Chetan has used cricket as a metaphor in the novel. Govind, Ishaan and Omi are all Hindus but they are ready to kill and die to save Ali, a Muslim youngster who may play for *Team India* one day. Ishaan kills many Hindus with fire bombs and gas blasts but will not hand Ali over to the Hindu mobs. He persuades his friends to save Ali.

> 'Ish, can I offer a bit of logic in the current chaos,' I said.
>
> 'What? We have no time,' Ish said.
>
> 'I know. But I also know what will happen if we
> fight thirty people. We will all die. They will get
> Ali and kill him too,' I said.
>
> 'So what are you tring to say,' Ish said and stood up.
>
> 'Giving up three lives to possibly save one.
> can you show me the maths in this?'
>
> 'Fuck your maths. This isn't about business.'
>
> 'Then what is it about? Why should we all die?
> Only because you love the kid?'
>
> 'No,' he said and turned his back to me.
>
> 'Then what?'
>
> 'Because he is a national, treasure.' Ish said.
>
> (*3Mistakes,* 230) (Emphasis added)

In the clash that follows Ishaan is wounded but Omi is killed. Govind repents for his cowardice in saving Ali and later pays for his treatment and makes up for his momentary fear. Cricket is presented as a saviour of communal unity in strife-torn India. In such moments Chetan Bhagat rises from a mere entertainer to a serious social activist who feels for his country and wants to heal long-festering wounds. *3 Mistakes* is a best-seller but it functions as on eye-opener for Chetan's young audience and exhorts them to move beyond divisive politics towards the concept of national integration.

National integration is again the theme of Chetan Bhagat's fourth novel, *2 States*, which is semi-autobiographical. In this work Bhagat has fictionalized his own bitter-sweet experiences when he a Punjabi, fell in love with a Tamil girl while studying at the IIM Ahmedabad, and wanted to marry her. India is a land of many cultures and languages, where inter-caste and inter-state marriages are frowned upon as rebellious acts. How depressing and frightening was the protagonist's mutiny against social taboos remains the central theme of the novel. The author's blurb puts the whole issue in perspective. All over the world marriage involves three steps:

> Boy loves girl. Girl loves boy.
>
> They get married.
>
> In India there are a few more steps.
>
> Boy loves girl.
>
> Girl loves boy.
>
> Girl's family has to love boy.
>
> Boy's family has to love girl.
>
> Girl's family has to love boy's family. Boy's family has to love girl's family. Girl and boy still love each other. They get married.
>
> Welcome to *2 States*, a story about Krish and Ananya who are from two different states of India, deeply in love and want to get married. Of course, their parents don't agree. To convert their love story into a love marriage, the couple have a tough battle in front of them. For it is easy to fight and rebel, but much harder to convince. Will they make it?[3]

Chetan Bhagat magnanimously dedicated this book to his in-laws. He admits that book is inspired by his own experiences and yet he requests the book be treated as fiction. Its hard to, considering every second couple in this country undergoes similar experiences. Not to mention every Bollywood movie harps on same theme.

The book is all about an IIMA couple's struggle to marry over the cultural differences. Krish is north Indian Punjabi boy in love with Tamilian Brahmin girl, Ananya. (Chetan Bhagat too is a Punjabi and his wife is a South Indian). The only catch is, Krish and Ananya don't want to elope or be estranged to their families, they choose to convince their parents for the marriage.

Both Ananya and Krish take turns to win over each other's families and then they try to make both the families like each other. After all in India, you don't marry the guy (or girl for that matter), you have to marry the family. In fact, Krish does get four gold rings made to propose to the girl's entire family! Sounds cheesy? Well, irrespective of a shortened plot summary, you must concede it is a mammoth project to accomplish anywhere, in real life.

Of course, it goes without saying that even though both Krish and Ananya are exception to their North Indian and South Indian clan; this book is a perfect opportunity to dwell into age-old North India versus South India divide.

Krish may be a Punjabi boy, but he is blissfully unaware how, in his community, greedy and offensive boy's side can be come on the girl's side during a Punjabi wedding. Similarly, Ananya, the Tamilian girl is completely unlike other Tamil girls: For one she is not as dark as southern girls (a fact she will be reminded over and over again by Krish's Punjabi clan) and unlike her staunch family, she both drinks and eats meat.

Though the premise is most realistic, it draws one's attention to cultural differences in diverse India. Some of them are as simple as boisterous, loud Punjabi music versus quiet, mellifluous Tamilian Carnatic music. However, the difference in sensibilities is predictable.

The initial pages of the book are set up at IIM Ahmedabad, Krish and Ananya meet in the canteen for the first time and eventually over a few days of combined study, fall in love. Life is great for them until their families meet each other. It takes sometime before they realize that they have a real problem at hand. Krish's mother needs the honour and gifts as due for boy's family. Ananya's parents insult the Punjabi woman as rustic and uncultured. The poor lovers dance to their tunes but the first meeting of the families ends in a fiasco.

2 States is a cunning combination of wish-fulfillment fantasy and matrimonial voyeurism. Much as Chetan Bhagat protests that this is purely a work of fiction, he doesn't mind holding out the promise of a peep into the travails he and his girlfriend underwent, trying to convince their respective families, before they became man and wife. The novel is a friendly, encouraging wink at India's mass of lovelorn youngsters confronted with a choice between parental wrath (in smaller towns, much more than wrath) and broken hearts. A net interview analyses the culture-clash in the novel:

> Recalling his own experience, Bhagat says: 'For my parents, the number one sticking point was that she is South Indian.' As a 'South Indian' myself, I can't help but gag at this all-too-familiar clumping of four states into one. 'Did they have a problem with her being a South Indian or with her being a Tamilian?' I ask. 'They didn't care. For them, it was all the same. 'From her side also, the biggest reservation was that I was not a Brahmin and I was not a Tamilian.'
>
> Bhagat laughs as he remembers how both their families felt their child had been trapped by the other. 'We were the quintessential, over-achieving middle-class kids. Both of us went to IIM, held lucrative jobs. Our parents should've been okay with whatever we did because we had done a lot of things right! Instead it made them feel worse—they felt that because their child has done so well, he/she deserved someone good from their own community. In my case, my family had the additional chip of being the boy's side.
>
> 'And a very well-qualified boy, too, who had a great market—it's rare to find a Punjabi boy who's IIT-IIM.'
>
> Considering that they were both financially independent, couldn't they have easily gone ahead and married against their families' wishes? 'We could have,' admits Bhagat. 'But we didn't want to shove the decision down their throats. It's easy to fight but very hard to convince.'
>
> And his novel, too, he adds, is about winning people over. And overcoming prejudices. Thanks to his marriage to a Tamilian, Bhagat was forced to confront his own preconceptions about South Indians and accept cultural differences. His biggest problem was that he found Tamil Brahmins to be puritanical and

closed. Closed to what? 'Closed to emotions, unlike Punjabis, who like to express themselves, and do so boisterously.' He illustrates his claim with an example.

> 'Tamilians will discuss the nuclear non-proliferation treaty within the family. But they won't openly express their feelings for each other. Even dancing among Punjabis is for fun. But for Tamils, it's 'Bharatnatyam', which is serious business. You don't laugh when you're doing it. I used to find all this strange, but now I've accepted that this is just the way they are.'4

Humour is Chetan Bhagat's forte and he has used his vision cleverly to expose the faultlines of his own Punjabi community that is boisterous as well as undereducated. Punjabis flaunt their wealth and are proud of their fair complexion, though they rarely work to keep their physique. Bhagat takes a peep at his native Delhi colonies of the Punjabi noveau riche. Actually Krish's mom has taken him to a rich family for him to bob at a prospective bride, Dolly:

> 'Don't stop our daughter from looking beautiful, Pammi-ji,' my mother said. Yes, Dolly was already ours.
>
> 'Who knows ji about whose daughter she will become? We only have two girls, everything is theirs,' Pammi said and spread her arms to show everything. Yes, the sofas, hideous marble coffee tables, curios, fans, air conditioners-everything belonged to the daughters and their future husbands. I have to say, for a second the thought of owning half this house made me wonder if my mother was right. But the next second the thought of losing Ananya came to me. No, I wouldn't give up Ananya for all the cashews and cash in the world. If only Pammi aunty allowed me to live in this house with Ananya.
>
> Dolly came scurrying down the steps with her perfume reaching us three seconds before her. 'Hello Aunty-ji,' Dolly said and went on to give my mother a tight hug.
>
> 'How beautiful our daughter has become!' my mother exclaimed.

> Dolly and I greeted each other with slight nods. She wore a wine red salwar kameez with vertical gold stripes running down it. She was abnormally white, and my mother was right; she did remind me of milk. She sucked in her stomach a little, though she wasn't fat. Her ample bosom matched Pammi aunty's and it made me wonder how these women would ever wean their children off without suffocating them.
>
> 'What are you saying? You haven't come at meal time, so I just arranged some heavy snacks. Raju, get the snacks. And get both the red and green chutneys!' she shrieked to her servant.
>
> Raju and another servant brought in a gigantic tray with samosas, jalebis, chole-bhature, milkcake, kachoris and, of course, the red and green chutneys. Twenty thousand calories were plonked on the table.
>
> 'You shouldn't have!' my mother said as she signalled the servant to pass the jalebis.
>
> 'Nothing ji, just for tasting. You should have come for dinner.'
>
> I felt I would come across as a retard if I didn't talk to Dolly now. **'what computer course are you doing?'**
>
> 'Microsoft Word, Power Point, Email, I don't know, just started. Looks quite hi-fi.'
>
> (2 *Stakes,* 62-63) (Emphasis added)

Krish is confused if he is going to marry a girl or a kothi with a petrol pump thrown in. His mother keeps pestering him, but he escapes by seeking a posting as a bank officer in Chennai. Thus he manages to return to Ananya, but visiting a Tam Brahm home is more of a cultural shock for the ignorant North Indian brat. Punjabi homes are noisy with lots of jokes and invectives thrown in. Actually Krish's parents are fighting all the time and his house echoes with shouts. Often Krish also joins the verbal duels and, as he confesses before a Guru at Aurobindo Ashram in Pondicherry, he once beat up his father when he was thrashing his mother. This story of Krish's parents is the darker thread in the novel. However, his first visit to Ananya's house is a virtual culture-shock.

> I stepped inside and handed him the gift pack.
>
> 'Shoes!' he said in a stern voice when I had expected 'thanks'.
>
> 'What?' I said.
>
> He pointed at the shoe rack outside the house.
>
> I removed my shoes and checked my socks for smells and holes. I decided to take them off, too. I went inside.
>
> 'Don't step on the rangoli', he warned.
>
> I looked down. My right foot rested on a rice flour flower pattern. 'Sorry, I am really sorry, sir,' I said and bent down to repair the pattern.
>
> 'It's OK. It can't be fixed now,' he said and ushered me into the living room. The long rectangular room looked like what would be left if a Punjabi drawing room was robbed. The sofas were simple, with cushions thinner than Indian Railways sleepers had, and formed the opposite of the decadent red velvet sofas of Pammi aunty. The walls had a pale green distemper finish. There were pictures of various South Indian gods all around the room. The dining area had floor seating. At one corner, there was a daybed with a tambura (which looks like a sitar) kept on it. An old man sat there. I wondered if Ananya's parents were cool enough to arrange live music for dinner.
>
> 'Sit,' Ananya's father said, pointing at the sofa.
>
> We sat opposite each other as I faced Ananya's dad for the first time in my life. I strained my brain hard for a suitable topic. 'Nice place,' I said.
>
> 'What is nice? No water in this area,' uncle said as he picked up a newspaper.
>
> I hung my head, as if to apologise for the water problem in Mylapore.

> Uncle opened the newspaper, which blocked his face from mine. I didn't know if it was intentional. I kept quiet and turned to the man with the tambura. I smiled, but he didn't react. The house had an eerie silence. A Punjabi house is never this silent even when people sleep at night.
>
> I bent forward to see if uncle was reading the paper or avoiding me. He had opened the editorial page of *the Hindu*. He read an opinion piece about AIADMK asking the government to do an inquiry on the defence minister who had sacked the naval chief. **It was heavy-duty stuff.**
>
> (2 *States*, 89) (Emphasis added)

Krish tries his best to win over Ananya's family. He gives tuitions to their young son, teaches her father how to make power-point presentations on a computer, and gives a push to her mother's singing career by inviting her to a bank concert. But nothing really works and Krish takes a posting back to New Delhi. In the meanwhile Ananya's family plans to arrange her marriage with a NRI groom who works in the U.S.A.

However, Ananya follows him to Delhi and impresses Krish's family with her bold and courageous attempt to save a marriage right at the wedding night when the groom's family asks for a bigger dowry. It is Krish's estranged father who visits Chennai to mend the broken relations and to finalize the Krish-Ananya marriage.

More fun and confusion follows when Krish's wedding party *(Baraat)* reaches Chennai. The Punjabis are totally at sea in the Tamilian ambience where they are supposed to go:

> 'What is the address?' Rajji mama said.
>
> I took out the piece of paper Ananya's dad had given me.
>
> 'I can't read this,' Rajji mama said.
>
> I took the paper back. It said:
>
> Arulmigu Kapaleewarar Karpagambal Thirumana Mandapam

> 16, Venkatesa Agraharam Street, Mylapore, Chennai.
>
> After three attempts at reading it, I had a headache. I counted the letters, my wedding venue had fifty alphabets in it. Delhi never gets this complicated. One of my older cousins had her wedding in Batra Banquets, another one in Bawa Hall.
>
> We struggled for twenty minutes on the streets of Mylapore before we reached the venue. Fortunately, the locals had abbreviated the name of the place to AKKT Mandapam. From actors to political parties to wedding halls, Tamilians love to keep complicated names first and then make acronyms for the same.
>
> (2 *States*, 251) (Emphasis added)

After some more hilarious misadventures the marriage is over and Krish' and Ananya's family sit for a feast. Here Ananya's father makes a speech that brings out the real significance of the fable. 2 *States* are not just two parts of India; they are the *two states of the human mind* that has to choose between love and hatred. He says:

> 'But we forget that this has happened because your child had love to give to someone in this world. Is that such a bad thing? Where did the child learn to love? From us, after all, the person they loved first is you.'
>
> Ananya clasped my arm and clenched it tight. The crowd listened with full attention.
>
> 'Actually, the choice is simple. When your child decides to love a new person, you can either see it as a chance to hate some people—the person they choose and their families. Which is what we did for a while. However, you can also see it as a chance to love some more people. And since when did loving more people become a bad thing?'
>
> He paused to have a glass of water and continued. 'Yes, the *Tamilian* in me is a little disappointed. But the *Indian* in me is quite happy. And more than anything, the human being in me is happy. After all,

> we've decided to use this opportunity to create more loved ones for ourselves.'
>
> When he kept the mike down, Ananya hugged him hard. The crowd burst into applause. Ananya and I cut the cake through the resounding claps. We fed each other and our respective in-laws a piece. The cameraman gathered both sets of parents for a picture.
>
> 'Ananya, see, both our parents. They are smiling,' I said.
>
> (2 *States,* 266) (Emphasis added)

The denouement is enthralling with Punjabis and Tamilians dancing and singing together in a scene of spontaneous revelry:

> Rajji mama avoided a bad fall while trying a particularly difficult *bhangra-break dance* fusion step to impress my new relatives. My cousins pushed me and Ananya together for a close dance. I held Ananya to me as we moved on the dance floor.
>
> 'Ananya,' I whispered in her ear.
>
> 'What?' she said softly.
>
> 'I love you and your father and your mother and your brother and your relatives.' I said.
>
> 'I love you and your clan, too,' she said.
>
> We kissed as Tamils and Punjabis danced around us.
>
> 'So, the self-imposed exile is over now? You said we'll only do it when we cross the finish line,' I said.
>
> 'Is that all you men think about?' she said.
>
> 'Only for the sake of uniting the nation,' I said.
>
> (2 *States,* 267) (Emphasis added)

The point that the novel is not only about geography but also about human psyche is reinforced by Krish's experience at Aurobindo Ashram in Pondicherry. Krish is angry, disenchanted and depressed when he is confronted with a Guru there. His heart is overburdened with his violent clash with his father and the Guru asks him to confess.

Reluctantly Krish recalls the dart night when he had hit his father:

> I shook my head at him, my eyes staring right into his. I slapped his face once, twice, then I rolled my hand into a fist and punched his face.
>
> My father went into a state of shock, he could't fight back. He didn't expect this; all my childhood I'd merely suffered his dominance. Today, it wasn't just about the broken glass. It wasn't only that the girl I loved would be gone. It was a reaction to two decades of abuse. Or that's how I defended it to myself. For how else do you justify hitting your own father? At that moment I couldn't stop, I punched his head until he collapsed on the floor. I couldn't remember the last time I revelled in violence like this. I was a studious child who stayed with his books all his life. Today, I was lucky there wasn't a gun at home.
>
> (2 *States*, 167) (Emphasis added)

The Guru advises him to follow the path of forgiveness for all those who have wronged him:

> 'I'll give you just one word to apply in your life.'
>
> 'What?'
>
> 'Forgiveness.'
>
> 'Meaning? You want me to forgive my father? I can't.'
>
> 'Why not?'
>
> 'Because what he did was so wrong. He has ruined my mother's life. He has never loved me.'
>
> 'I am not saying he did the right thing. **I am asking you to forgive him.**'
>
> 'Why?'
>
> 'For you. Forgiving doesn't make the person who hurt you feel better, it makes you feel better.'
>
> I pondered over his words.

> 'Close your eyes again,' Guruji said. 'Imagine you have bags on your head. They are bags of anger, pain and loss. How do they feel?'
>
> 'Heavy,' I sighed.
>
> 'Remove them from your head one by one,'
>
> Guruji said. 'Imagine you are wearing a thick cloak that is wearing you down. Pardon the hurt others have caused you. What they did is past. What is bothering you today are your current feelings that come from this load. Let it go.'
>
> Strange as Guruji's metaphors were, I felt compelled to obey the imagery in my mind. My head felt lighter.
>
> 'And surrender to God,' he went on. 'You don't control anything or anyone.'
>
> 'I don't understand,' I said.
>
> 'Do you control your life?' Your life depends on so many internal organs functioning right. You have no control on them, if your lungs don't cooperate. If your kidneys fail, if your heart stops, it is all over, You'll drop dead now. God has chosen to give you the gift of life, surrender to him.'
>
> He kept me in meditation for the next few minutes. 'And now, you are free to go,' Guruji smiled.
>
> (2 *States*, 168-69) (Emphasis added)

These are the words that change *the states of the human mind*. Anger grows into compassion, hatred into love. Once man realizes that God's will is supreme, all disappointments and difference sink into the peace of faith. Janina Gomes writes:

> Wrestling with God always and inevitably has a positive outcome. We become freer from within. We begin to see a meaning in conflicts and confrontation. When up against a wall, be sure God will meet us in the very impasse we are in. He confronts us, not in the inhuman way some people do, but with deference to

> our independence and respect for our deepest longings and desires.
>
> Confrontation in real life is unavoidable. Confrontation if handled badly can lead to conflict. Conflict arises from difference and the inability of people to integrate this diversity. Conflict hampers full development because very often it is rooted in the past as unfinished business. A history of non-acceptance, of claims and counterclaims, of greed, jealousy, of disrupted social interactions, sometimes ending in violence and war can all make conflicts difficult to resolve and lead to an emotional overload.
>
> Generations of people pass on the same hatreds from the past. They have been and continue to be at loggerheads. Acrimony and bad taste, attacks and counter-attacks. We are familiar with it all. On the other hand negotiated settlements require wisdom, detachment, statesmanship, a certain give and take, exploration of the unfamiliar and breaking of new ground.
>
> If we allow the grace of God to flow unimpeded in us, we will find that goodness flows naturally from us, like the river. Others will find refuge and solace in us and we will become messengers of God without great effort.
>
> Time will be on our side. Nature will support and help us. We will walk confidently in the future. The God we evaded will flood our lives with His grace. And after a while we will find that there is no need to wrestle any more. God will be our all in all. Was that not the reason why we were born?[3]

This is how the *state* of Punjab joins the *state* of Tamilnadu, the *state* of anger grows into happiness, the *stated* hatred changes into love, the *state* of confrontation transforms into the *state* of celebration. And the epilogue shows the fruition of this union between *two states:*

> The doctor took out the whole baby.

'Thank you, doctor, thank you so much,' I said emotionally and moved to shake his hand.

'Wait,' the doctor said through his masked face.

'What,' Ananya said.

'I don't know,' I said. 'Oh wait, there's another leg. Wow, there's another boy.'

'Twins?' she said in disbelief, looking ready to faint.

'Yes,' the doctor said, 'Congratulations.'

The nurse cleaned up the two babies and gave them to me.

'Be careful,' she said as I took one in each arm.

'You are from two different states, right? So, what will be their state? the nurse said and chuckled.'

'They'll be from a state called India,' I said.

(*2 States*, 268-69) (Emphasis added)

One can conclude this analysis with reference to an interview posted on Chetan Bhagat's website where he talks about his latest novel:

Q. What is *2 States* about?

A. *2 States* is about a boy and a girl from two different states of India, who fall in love and want to get married. Of course, their parents don't agree. What happens next is what the book is about.

Q. The tagline says the story of my marriage. Is it inspired by real events?

A. Well, like my first book, this book draws a lot of inspiration from my own life. I am Punjabi and my wife is Tamilian, similar to the protagonists in the story. Rest, I leave it for the reader to figure it out.

Q. Love and Marriage—why did you decide to write this book after the relatively intense *3 mistakes of my life*?

A. Writing *3 mistakes* became too heavy for me. A story about riots, manipulative politics and the impact on the younger generation made me quite disturbed after writing the novel. Also, my strength is humour and many of my readers felt the book becoming more serious. So, I am back to doing something light and fun—but still with a message.

Q. What is the message?

A. I'd like people to read the book to find it out for themselves. However, the message is simple—if India is one country, why can't we marry a boy/girl from another state? A modern India will never emerge with so many differences between people.

Q. Are you nervous before the release given the extraordinary expectations?

A. Of course I am nervous as the size of the print runs is unheard of in Indian publishing. The book has to deliver to these expectations. However, two things make me more relaxed. One, the initial feedback from editors is highly positive and two, I feel secure about my reader's love for me. If I won't let them down, they won't either.

Q. Any message for your readers?

A. More than anything, thanks a lot. Most of my readers are young and I'll say, always try to look at the brighter side of life, even in the toughest of times. This attitude makes us surmount the biggest challenges, just as the characters do in my books. And keep love above everything else in life.[6]

Notes

1. Chetan Bhagat: *The 3 Mistakes of My Life* (Delhi, Rupa, 2008) p.78 (Emphasis added) (All subsequent citations are from this edition and the page nos. have been given in parenthesis)
2. Swami Sukhbodhananda: 'Of Success And Failure', New Delhi, *The Times of India*, April 6, 2011, p. 14.
3. Chetan Bhagat: *2 States* (Delhi, Rupa, 2009) Back cover page blurb. (All subsequent citations are from this edition and the page no's have been given in parenthesis)
4. Net entry: www.chetanbhagat.com/blog
5. Janina Gomes: 'Wrestling with God' Delhi, *The Times of India*, July 27, 2010. p.10 (Emphasis added)
6. Net entry: www. chetanbhagat.com/blog

5

Chetan Bhagat's Protagonists As Angry Young Men

The angry decade of 1950's marks a watershed in the history of contemporary English literature. The creators of the cult anti-hero broke down the division between elitist high-brow and popular middle-brow fiction. The term Angry Young Man originates from the title of Leslie Allen Paul's autobiography that appeared in 1951. However, it became a cult-figure, a critical catch-phrase, with the popularity of John Osborne's *Look Back in Anger* (1956). Three British novelists—Kingsley Amis, John Wain, and John Braine—also contributed to the growth of the angry phenomena with their ironic, anti-establishment fictional creations. The first to appear was John Wain's Charles Lumley in *Hurry on Down* (1953), a rambling picaresque novel where the protagonist keeps redefining his identity in class-terms. A close second was Kingsley Amis' *Lucky Jim* (1954), where the hero, Jim Dixon, plays a hundred tricks to cock a snook at the very class structure that he hopes to join at the creamy layer. The next important novel of anger is John Braine's *Room at the Top* (1957), whose hero, Joe Lampton, is a shameless social climber who uses his sex appeal to win the daughter of a rich man and thus advance his career a few notches.

The angry novels have as their theme the striving of their protagonists to escape from the negative aspects of their class. They wish to exclude poverty, narrowness, lack of status and desire to achieve the wealth, education or respect that is associated with the middle class. Men like them succeed but they pay a high price for it. These novels show that the successful characters forget close contact with the family and neighbours. They lead lives of great tension.

> The tensions and contradications between the roots and aspirations can become a long term problem for those who have moved out of their class and for the family that has been left behind; there is no blue-print for how it should be solved. In the first place the individual is involved in a lengthy process of weighing the pros and cons of the two life-styles—community against individualism, or emotions against intellect. At the same time, he is aware that his own development is being in turn, weighed by his family. Is he still the hero of the class, the pioneer, beating them at their own game, or is he getting above himself; becoming one of them as opposed to remaining one of us? Thirdly, he is trying to come to terms with his new class, to be accepted without being compromised, to be more than a token figure or an eternal outsider.1

Thus the character suffers from complete isolation. Neither can he go back to the strata he has just left nor can he fully adjust with the new class he has attempted to become a part of. In the novels of John Wain too, the heroes suffer from a deep sense of isolation and loneliness. Charles Lumley, the protagonist of *Hurry on Down* leaves university and then he journeys through Britain holding a variety of jobs as window washer, smuggler, hospital orderly, chauffeur and bouncer in a shoddy night club respectively, because he is not ready to accept the boundaries of class.

Charles Lumley enjoys his work of window-washing but his sister-in-law and her husband Robert (who represent Charles's own class) despise him because Charles has adopted the labour class way of living and doesn't put on the uniform indicating his own status. Thus discarded by his own people he seeks asylum in a bar. There also, he is unable to adjust with the people. His personality had been shaped in a manner which would suit a middle class environment. Now at this age, influences of his upbringing and education have become so inseparable from his personality under the heavy layers of training from his childhood to his youth that he is unable to adjust in the atmosphere of the labour class. He had been deprived of his sting and his sharp edges had been cut as the middle class decorum demanded. In contrast to which the reality of the lower class is that life is to be snatched, the survival instinct so to say and therefore children are so nurtured that they may grab the utmost possibilities from this world. For this, they need to get on with all sorts of roughness in manners without hesitation, which is lacking in Charles Lumley.

Charles is thus caught in a dilemma. He wants to move up the social ladder but he is fond of the warm relationships that exist in the working classes. The contrary pulls on his life are evident in these lines.

> He had always resisted the idea of collaboration for he had not dared to hope for a partner who would be without the simple heavy curiosity of the provincial working class. He had imagined himself being pumped and dreaded, having his dead past raked up as a spy in an enemy country dreads interrogation. For the rest of the life he was to travel without passport and it was important not to be held for questioning.[2]

Charles Lumley's society of origin has its magnetic pull for him as at times it can be seen, for example, in his affair with Veronica—where he gets a little solution and solace from the complicated riddles of his life.

With the discovery that his friend's wife (Betty) has to satiate the physical lust of some other person to feed her husband (with whom Charles was staying then) he realizes that he has become a parasite on the world the detested. The interwoven complications of this world and the complications of Charles's life have been very intellectually brought before us in the following passage:

> The network everywhere; no a web, sticky and cunningly arranged. You were either a spider, sitting

> comfortably in the middle or waiting with malicious joy in hiding, or you were a fly, struggling amid the clinging threads. (*Hurry on,* 76)

Despite his best efforts, Lumley is never successful in ignoring the inevitability of social stratification. In his third job of hospital orderly he observes the pyramid shaped society—at the top of which were doctors and a few senior nurses—matrons and sisters, next came the nurses in general and at the bottom were the cooks, technicians, clerical and domestic workers. Charles found his place somewhere near the bottom.

He gets a bigger jolt in his bitter dialogue with Burge at a party:

> Just what the bloody hell do you think you're playing at Lumley, eh? They tell me you've taken a job at the hospital as an orderly. Carrying buckets about and emptying bedpans. What the bloody hell's the big idea.
>
> 'Do I understand Burge' he said with a hint of a choke in his voice, 'That you are interfering with my right, the absolute right of a citizen, to do just whatever work I may choose? (*Hurry on,* 164)

Charles tells the men at the party that he despises them on two counts:

> First because my education which you throw in my face, was an education along humane lines that didn't leave me with any illusions about the division of human beings into cricket teams called classes, and secondly because while you've been living this mean life of—of good mixing, beer drinking, and slapping the nurses' bottoms on night duty, I've been out, out in the world Learning the truth about things—and what is more. (*Hurry on,* 166)

Whenever Charles is distressed, he seeks asylum in women. Earlier it was Veronica and now—that he is again disturbed by the fact that he still represents a class—there is Rosa in whose arms he may forget all his tensions. As soon as he is out of any tension he did not need women anymore, neither Veronica, nor

Rosa. In his quest he switches over to another job of a chauffeur.

The presence of Mr. Hutchins in the novel stands in contrast against Charles Lumley. Hutchins used to be ashamed of his parents in school because they had labour class appearance. The juxtaposition of Hutchins—who has adopted a tutor's job (a middle class occupation) and Charles Lumley (who as a chauffeur has been given the task of receiving him at the station) is remarkable in the following passage which must be quoted extensively in order to fully realise the mental working of Lumley:

> The very existence of Hutchins, within five miles of himself, was an insult. He decided to be offensive-Hutchins turned round, irresolute. Charles folded his peaked cap and hid it carefully in his pocket. In his brown suit he had nothing about him to suggest the chauffeur. Just in time Hutchins had spotted him.
>
> 'Well this is a surprise Lumley,' he said, coming up the platform. 'I'm astonished,' said Charles. 'I'm doing some tutoring for a family down here,'
>
> 'And you can't have too many friends and patrons among the rich. It all helps'.
>
> Hutchins flushed dully. 'If you're implying that my motive in tutoring is an unworthy one, of course, I----
>
> 'Not at all. Social climbing isn't unworthy. When a man's got half-way up the ladder by hard work, as you have, it's only human for him to decide that he might as well jump the rest of the rungs by a quicker method.
>
> (*Hurry on*, 193-94)

But immediately after Hutchins comes to know that Charles himself was the driver of the car which was meant to take him to his destination he reacts:

> 'Well Lumley, I'm sorry you're down on your luck, I should have thought you could have got a better job than this I didn't think you would have come down to this.' 'What do you mean come down' 'I could give you

> a recommendation that would probably get you a job in a prep, school. That would be a start at least.'
>
> 'Listen Goerge:' Charles said wearily. 'Never mind the missionary zeal. I don't want honest work. I'm like you, I prefer to be a parasite. A louse on the scalp of society.' 'I don't see the comparison, I must,' said Hutchins stiffly. 'What could be plainer? I drive the great man's car. You try to tinker with the brain-box of his son'. (*Hurry on,* 195)

Charles is not able to stay in the chauffer's job also, because his softer heart motivates him to take the responsibility of a damage to the car upon himself—just to save his master's son: who actually had committed the mistake. Charles's conscience tells him that:

> We knew you wouldn't be staying,
>
> You're not the type. (*Hurry on,* 212)

Charles cannot totally ignore the society around him. In each job he undertakes he has to put himself in relation to particular class. Even when he is a chauffeur he is totally aware of his dependence on the people of a distinguished class, an awareness which he intends to avoid and then he is reminded of a line: 'And I a twister love that I abhor.'

Finally, Charles confesses that he cannot escape from the complex character of society and its class structure and that his feelings cannot be absolutely pure; it must have some alloy. When he leaves his job as chauffeur at the industrialist's Hampshire house he realises that:

> The people he belonged with were ill, disgusting, unsuccessful, comic, but still alive, still generating some kind of human force.
>
> This expensive bucolic string had offered nothing more than an escape down a blind alley, and it had taken a crack-brained mechanic, a nymphomaniac, and a deranged careerist to show him that. As ever, the serious point had emerged through the machinery of the ludicrous. His life was a dialogue, full of deep and

> tragic thoughts, expressed in hoarse shouts by red-nosed music hall comics. (*Hurry on,* 223)

In his gag-writing job Charles has enough time to think about himself in relation to others and in the end he agrees to retain his original self in this highly organized materialistic world. Charles discovers in his journey that to preserve the dignity of personal and humane is the greatest morality.

The job of gag-writing is best suited to him as it finally places him as a part of the commercial middle class. But his journey earns him an advantage of insight over others which he could not have acquired, if he had automatically moved to his bestowed position.

So here the hero is not a very enterprising youth, accomplishing heroic tabs and gaining everybody's admiration and co-operation thereby. Gindin aptly states:

> Since the end of world war II, the unheroic figure has become the standard fictional representation of the age. Without a rigid class structure enabling him to display his vitrue by romantic opposition without any publicly fixed definition of viture at all, the would be exceptional and heroic figures had become the fool, the man living in terms of on outmoded ideal or a hollow pretence.[3]

Under such circumstances it is but natural that the oppressed character looks for emotional outlet. The easiest he can resort to is love where he gets a partner to share his feelings and his emotions. In Wain's novels, the characters resort to love in moments of emotional crises. Charles Lumley doesn't want to take root in the society and wishes to be left alone to grow naturally into his true self. In his attempt to escape a degenerated society he faces many problems. To cope with his frustrations he needs the support of love and the lap of a woman. When he thinks about his situation and finds no solution to the problems he feels a need to go to his wife Sheila:

> The need to see her which he had fiercely repressed for months, flared up in his body and brain as the bus

> crawled through the leaf green Lanes; it was so much what he needed—a return, a recognition, a point of rest, which yet involved recriminations and no immediate practical decisions. But this peace was still to be won, and the violence of his inner tension caught and shook him fiercely as he walked up the garden path. (*Hurry on*, 8-9)

The manifestation of Charles' passionate craving for his wife in the above passage is one example of Wain's master-hand in expressing human emotions. John Wain was all along conscious of the moral aspects in life. He tried his best to maintain a sense of morality in his novels. Yet, he could not shun reality. He studied society for the themes of his novels. While writing about love and romance Wain wanted to be realistic, so his heroes are not completely moral. They do have a tendency to fall out of the arena of morality. They sometimes indulge in love affairs with more than one woman.

> Wain is both more of a moralist and more of a romantic than Amis, and his observation of life is passionately coloured, indeed sometimes distorted, by his moral convictions.[4]

Charles often tries to beep himself busy in one occupation or the other to resist any of the badges of status which Englishmen generally impose upon one another but he is nowhere untouched by this imposition. The other girl under whose charm Charles is relieved of some of his tensions is Veronica. Veronica is a romantic heroine. Her uncle does not allow her to have a love affair with Charles; so in her uncle's absence Veronica requests Charles to take her for an outing. Charles takes her to his cottage. They sat in the garden, went to the river, even at night they had stayed there.

Charles has purity of sentiments in his love for Veronica. He expresses his intention to marry her but Veronica is not prepared. His real feeling is expressed when the group of smugglers with whom Charles worked had been identified by a journalist and the group together were murdering the journalist. Charles was trying to save him but he was already dead. Now alongwith others Charles had to escape from the eyes of the police. All this created much pressure upon his mind. Charles was thinking about his changed character and sought shelter in Veronica.

In his attitude to love Wain indulges in psychoanalysis. He looks at his characters not only from the external or physical point of view but devices into the deep recesses of the mind simply in order to find out the reality. In *Hurry on Down* Wain gives many detailed descriptions of the working of the hero's mind when he encounters a new girl. *Hurry on Down,* thus is the saga of an angry young man in search for a career as well as a soul mate. Charles Lumley seems to have succeeded at both fronts, though the title of the novel does leave a question mark about his ultimate destination in life.

Kingsley Amis, born in South London in 1922, educated at the city of London School and St. John's College, Oxford, himself worked for a time as a university lecturer. Following the publication of *Lucky Jim,* now considered a modern classic, in 1954, he wrote over twenty novels, including *The Alteration* (1976), winner of the John W. Campbell Memorial Award, *The Old Devils* (1986), winner of the Booker Prize, and *The Biographer's Moustache* (1995), which was to be his last book. Malcolm Bradbury comments:

> Kingley Amis' *Lucky Jim*—a remarkably funny book which had been round sixteen publishers before it got into print in 1954 came to be the exemplary fifties novel.[5]

It shows anger in the acedemic corridors as Amis knew the situation very well for he himself had seen everything by his own eyes. Jim Dixon is a young history lecturer in a provincial university and he has to work under a tedious and ridiculous professor. From the very beginning of the novel we come to know how bored Jim feels in his company. His boss, Professor Welch, always tries to pose how superior he is, how right he is as if he knew everything. Welch is continuously talking about his concert without thinking a moment whether Dixon is interested or not. Dixon on the other hand comes near to wishing that they really are (talking History). At heart he just hates his professor and pulls faces behind his back.

Welch is totally unaware of Dixon's inner feelings. He continues talking and Dixon on the other side tries hard to flail his features into some sort of positive response. Why Dixon bends so much in front of such a ridiculous personality who is not worthy of anything, even of his post at a place like this? At heart he knows very well that all his future depends on this particular man.

> This man had decisive power over his future at any rate until the next four or five weeks up.[6]

It throws light upon the tortures that one has to face. Everything depends on the high authorities, they can appoint anybody or may dismiss one if they are not pleased. Knowledge does not count. Dixon cleverly tries to change the subject by asking about Margaret, who is his colleague. She had tried to commit suicide as she has failed in her love. Now she is living with the Welch's—Dixon himself knows everything but for just changing their subject matter, he asks about her. He wants to leave no chance of flattering his professor and says:

> I think living with you, professor, and Mrs. Welch must have helped her a lot to get out of the woods.
>
> (*Jim*, 9)

Welch feels very pleased to listen such words and adds:

> Yes I think there must be something about the atmosphere of the place, you know, that has some sort of healing effect. (*Jim*, 9)

After no more than a minor change of direction the misfiring vehicle of his conversation has been hauled back on to its usual course. Dixon feels just helpless fatigue. Welch has forgotten that he has invited him for tea at his home. And now Dixon is *angry*. It is so humiliating and insulting. He wishes to:

> pick up his professor round the waist, squeeze the furry grey blue waist coat to expel the breath-----and plunge the too small feet in their capless shoes into a lavatory basin, pulling the plug once, twice, and again stuffing the mouth with toilet papers.
>
> (*Jim*, 10) (Emphasis added)

He smiles dreamily, while thinking all this. Welch says that he will go up to collect his bag from his room. Dixon keeps on waiting and starts thinking of Margaret. Actually it was all by chance that he had to accept Margaret as his girl friend. She was senior to him, and it was quite natural to say 'yes' to a female lecturer when she invites him up for coffee. It was all just like a web of relationship from which it was not easy to come out. He was pulled into her business by a combination of virtues he had not known he possessed. Dixon is in quite a funny situation. A person, whose philosophy is to read as little as possible, is appointed as a lecturer, and is asked to prepare lectures on a subject that he just dislikes. Dixon's problem is that inwardly he doesn't believe in old values, in a particular moral code of conduct, but outwardly he has to show off that he is much cultured and believes in acedemic values. Dixon is always irritated. He is always at odds. What is the reason behind all this? Inwardly he is filled with anarchic fury. He deeply wants to react, to reject all the moral and conventional codes. He wants to be away from all this show off. His character highlights all the defects that are found in provincial universities or colleges. One is compelled to do what he never wishes and that is the root cause of all such humiliation. The high authorities think it their right to show they know too much of their culture.

Dixon just hates Welch and his charlatan circle. He believes in soberiety and simplicity. He has none of the qualities of the snobbish class, represented by Welch and his son, Bertrand, who is a painter. Their class is reflected in their language also. Dixon is unable to overcome his fury:

> He no longer wanted, for example, to inscribe on the departmental time-table a short account, well tricked out with obscenities, of his views on the Professor of History, the Department of History, medieval History, history and Margaret and hang it out of the window for the information of the passing students and lecturers, nor did he on the whole, now intend to tie Welch up in his chair and beat him about the head and shoulders with a bottle until he disclosed why,

> without being French himself, he'd given his sons French No, he'd just say, quite quietly and very slowly and distinctly, to give Welch a good chance of catching his general drift: look here, you old cockchafer, what makes you think you can run a history department even at a place like this, eh, you old cockchafer? I know what you'd be good at, you old cockchafer. (*Jim*, 85)

The reality is Dixon himself wants to leave all this, he is just seeking a chance. He makes fun of Welch while singing:

> 'you ignorant clod, you stupid old sod------you wordy old turdy old scum, you griping old piping old bum...
>
> (*Jim*, *87*) (Emphasis added)

His hatred of the elite class shows not real anger but envy. He gets his opportunity by the end of the novel when he outsmarts Bertrand and lands a cushy job as secretary to Gore-Urquhart, a millionaire. Simultaneously, he also attracts his girl-friend, Christine, to emerge a winner all the way. As he gets ready to leave for London, Christine comes running to meet him on the railway platform. She frankly tells him that she has finished with Bertrand. *A blur of happiness suffused Dixon's face.* (249). He tells her about his getting the job on which Bertrand had his eye. Dixon has finally won the battle:

> He thought what a pity it was that all his faces were designed to express rage or loathing.
>
> Now that something had happened which really deserved a face, he'd none to celebrate it with.
>
> (*Jim*, 250) (Emphasis added)

When he goes with Christine, the crowd of Welches come out and block the pavement but they pass in the midst of them laughing.

Jim who is inwardly and comically at odds with the Bloomsbury academic, artistic and social culture of his elders, embodies the powerful contemporary mood. *Lucky Jim* is a campus novel dealing with the jealousies and rivalries in small town universities that do not enjoy the status of Oxford or Cambridge. The novel shows the ambitions of the educated lower middle class youth. They have to face discrimination because of their humble origins. The superiority complex showed by the upper classes makes them angry. They feel that their merit is not respected because of the stigma of class. Dixon's antics work as a tool of social revolution. The element of satire has also been used to expose the shallowness and hypocrisy of the upper class men like Welch. They speak and behave as they only know what culture is. Class is reflected in every aspect of their lives, their standard of living, their possessions and their refined language.

Jim also realizes the hollowness of scholarship. He hates the snobbery of those who make a show of learning though he himself has to make similar presentations as a need for advancement in the job. His overdrinking, oversmoking and casual sex are the symptoms of his frustration and an attempt to avenge the humiliations inflicted upon him. His immorality is also related to his anger, his attempt to break all the rules imposed by the society. These acts reflect his desire for individual freedom in personal matters. He revolts against class prejudices. He proves that he is also worthy of anything; he is not an oddity in this society. If he is cheated, he will cheat the others. He thinks he has won, but he only wins by joining them. He does not defeat the upper class but joins them. There is no revolution sponsored by him but only personal success won by some play-acting and good luck. His anger does not seem genuine but only a drama to attain his ends.

The third name among the Angries is of John Braine who was born in Bradford in 1922, spent much of his young life at Thackley, a village technically part of Bradford but in spirit independent of it, and went to St. Bede's Grammar School, Bradford. After various dead-end job he became a library assistant at Bingley, a small town near Bradford, and followed this career with an interval of war service in the Royal Navy. However, the success of *Room at the Top* (1957) enabled him to devote his whole time to writing. His second novel *The Vodi* was published in 1959 and *Life at the Top,* a sequel to *Room at the Top,* in 1962. He wrote some other novels also like *The*

Jealous God (1964), *The Crying Game* (1968) and *Stay With Me Till Morning* (1970).

Though his other novels didn't enjoy much celebrity, *Room at the Top* is the defining work of his oeuvre. In this novel he very well expresses the pulse of the young generation in the 1950's. How they revolted against the class prejudices and how far they could go to get their ambitions fulfilled? In fact, they were those who showed their anger and revolted by gatecrashing into the same class they hated most. Actually by doing this they hit hard on the face of those who treated them as oddities in society. They always wanted to reach the Top but the question is are they happy after getting there? In fact, they are successful in getting or finding the room at the Top by losing the earth beneath.

The same is the case with Braine's protagonist, Joe Lampton in *Room at the Top*. He is bitterly conscious of his class, his humble breeding that makes him angry. He was born at Dufton and his career graph shows him as a junior clerk. He comes to Warley with high expectations and soon he becomes a part of the urban racket. He also becomes a virtual zombie, a person made of steel, a dead person. He marries a high class woman to achieve what he wants. But after getting this height he realizes that he has sold his independence to get an elusive success. He gets all his ambitions fulfilled at the cost of his real self, his real happiness, his true love and his sentiments and feelings and what ever peace of mind he had. At the end he feels nostalgia for old days, riches have not made him happy. He recalls his past that haunts him like a ghost every minute. He remembers when he came to Warley his face was not innocent but unused:

> By sex, by money by making friends and influencing people, hardly touched by any of the muck one's forced to wade through to get what one wants.[7]

He arranges his lodgings at Mrs. Thompson's and while going to hers' he feels a thrill that he is going to the Top. He feels as if he is moving into a different world that even from first brief glimpses fills him with excitement.

> ---- big houses with drives and orchards and manicured hedges---- expensive cars Bentleys, Lagondas---- parked everywhere in a kind of ostentatious litter as if the district had dropped them at random as evidence of its wealth... (*Room,* 10)

These are all symbols of Top and Joe feels enchanted by everything. He is continuously comparing Warley with Dufton. In Warley Cyprus Avenue is broad, straight and lined with cypresses while in Dufton the street Oak crescent didn't curve an inch and there was not a bush along it. Joe realizes----- as if all my life I'd been eating the sawdust and thinking it was bread. (*Room* 10)

Joe gets a chance to meet the upper class people when he goes to the local theatre. Here he meets a girl, Susan Brown, who impresses him as the ladder for social rise he has been seeking. He has got the girl, he is searching for, the grade two woman. Joe has a chance; after all he is gifted with a smart personality.

At heart Joe feels attraced to Susan who has a rich and adoring papa. Like Jimmy Porter who always wants his wife to wake up from her beauty sleep Joe desires Susan to be aware of human miseries. Joe comes to know through Eva that Susan has got tied up with Jack Wales, his boyfriend. He proves to be a social climber who is clever enough to use love and marriage as a ladder. He and Jim Dixon are like brothers in shrewdness. Joe phones Susan and fixes a meeting on Saturday night for the ballet. Joe's intentions are very clear, he pretends to love Susan and wants to marry her as she belongs to the right income group and has a lot of money. He thinks of her like a princess who is beautiful, lives in a golden palace, wears fine clothes, and rich jewels and eats chicken and cakes. She is grade two woman with whom he may marry and live happily ever after.

On the other hand his intimacy with Alice keeps on increasing day by day. He considers her nice and exciting, but lost, like a little girl looking for something. A genuine relationship is growing between him and her. Alice's husband George Aisgil is also the prey of Joe's hatred. The choice between Alice and Susan is the major dilemma in Joe's life.

Alice is mature, loving and faithful. She has taught Joe what love is. Susan, on the other hand, is a child-woman, a silly spoilt girl who does not know what true love is. But her father has loads of money and this tilts the balance in her favour. Joe shamelessly jilts Alice and goes for Susan.

Joe is fascinated with Susan as she is lucky, she has always been lucky, she's never known the reality of the cold bedroom. She has never had to worry about exams or a job or the price of new clothes, even her way of speaking with its touchingly childish affection is a luxury not one of the working classes can afford. Joe loves Susan not as a person but a means to join the upper class:

> I was taking Susan not as Susan, but as a *Grade A lovely,* as the daughter of a factory owner, as the means to obtaining the key to the Aladdin's cave of my ambitions as she was taking me as the perfect lover...
>
> (*Room,* 139) (Emphasis added)

A part of him feels a great tenderness for her, but the most important part of him is continuing the operation according to plan. When she asks him how much he loves her, he replies:

> A hundred thousand pound's worth. (*Room,* 140)

Joe is very happy as good fortune seems to be following him like a huge affectionate dog. He is called by Hoylake who indirectly threatens him that he should leave Susan or he may be sacked as councillors have the great power to affect the career of any official.

Joe is too angry as he is bitterly conscious of his class. That's the only reason why all people have power over him. The past chapters of his life start beating in his mind. He thinks that he lacks the necessary background, the poise, the breeding. He is essentially vulgur and possesses no talent. He has a relationship with a grade two woman who is of an ardent and impetuous nature, and lacks worldly experience which would enable her to deal firmly with a man of Joe Lampton's type.

Joe tries his best to seduce Susan and his plans succeed. One fine day her father phones him directly and invites him for lunch at Con Club. Joe thinks that Brown in some unpleasant indirect way, is going to kick him in the guts as what chance has the swineherd against the prince Jack Wales:

> Now it had come, it was actually a relief: there was no where I could retreat to, no need to be pleasant to anyone, I could afford the luxury of speaking my mind. (*Room,* 200)

When he enters the club he feels that it is the place where money grows, where decisions are taken, here is the place where the right word or smile or gesture can transport one into a higher grade overnight. It seems that the gates are opening for Joe into a different world step by step. Brown reaches the main point saying that he is thinking of setting him up in business. He may lend him what is necessary to buy a partnership somewhere on one condition that he would never meet Susan again. Joe very cleverly rejects his offer and stresses upon the fact that he loves Susan to the core of his heart and would marry her at any cost even against his will. Brown says that he won't do that as he is marrying her with her consent. Infact he is testing him if he is the right person for her daughter. His plan does work to perfection. He has come to know that Susan is pregnant. Brown tests him again when he says that he will send her to a nursing home as it is not too late, Joe is agitated again and threatens that he will go to the police. Brown says that he need not worry. He advises him to leave the Town Hall and Alice at once. Joe says that he has already left Alice. Now Joe has got everything he wanted, the luxuries of good fortune. He has arrived at the *Room at the Top*. He has also been included in the higher class:

> There was a handshake, there was talk of a contract, there was tolerance. I've been young and daft myself there was praise—you'r the sort of young man we want. There's always room at the top there was sternness.... ... all that I could say, again and again and again was the equivalent of those two syllables of shocked incredulity. (*Room,* 212)

Hearing of Joe's engagement with Susan Alice bills hereself, but Joe Lampton buries his remorse in the dreams of future luxury. His social climbing has reached its acme. Joe Lampton and Jim Dixon are similar type of protagonists who use love and marriage as a ladder to climb up social hierarchy and make room at the top. But there is a basic difference between the two, Jim is not guilty about anything like Joe whose soul is burdened with guilt complex that will not let him enjoy anything. In the words of Malcolm Bradbury:

> John Braine's *Room at the Top* (1957) is the story of Joe Lampton, who exploits his looks and his body to ensure his personal success and his greedy social ascent in the Yorkshire town of Leddersford and beyond.[8]

The angry young men may be classified as anti-establishment rebels, but their ranting seems to be a means for self-advancement. However, these figures emerged as catalysts in modern literature as they gave a great boost to the best-seller phenomenon. Not to speak of literature, these irreverent tradition-bashers became the archetype of the New Hero in films, theatre and television. In India, for example, Amitabh Bachchan emerged as the angry young man of films, raving and ranting against an unjust system that rewarded evil, while beating the villains at their own game of fraud or violence.

Chetan Bhagat's protagonists are Bachchan-like in their rage against a system that conspires to defeat them. Ryan Oberai, Vroom, Ishaan and Krish are all angry young men in their own right, refusing to make compromises that may reward them but bill their souls. They refuse to buy success at the cost of meek conformism to the dictates of a rotten system. They would rather choose the path of rebellion that may bring them to their knees for a while, but their heads are always held high. In this way, they differ from the British angries.

Consider Ryan, the central character in *Five Point Someone*. His anger comes to the fore in the very opening scene when his co-students are being inhumanly ragged by the seniors. He remains mute and obedient for a while, but once the seniors cross the limit, he explodes:

> Ryan smashed the two Coke bottles on the balcony parapet. Each bottle now was butt-broken, and he waved the jagged ends in air.
>
> 'Come, you bastards,' Ryan swore, his face scarlet like a watermelon slice. Baku and the demon retreated a few paces. Anurag, who had been smouldering in the backdrop, snapped to attention. 'Hey, cool it everyone here. How did this happen? What is your name—Ryan, take it easy man. This is just fun.'
>
> 'It's not fun for me,' growled Ryan, 'just get the hell out of here.'
>
> Alok and I looked at each other. I was hoping Ryan knew what he was doing. I mean sure, he was saving our ass from a Coke bottle, but broken Coke bottles could be a lot worse.
>
> 'Listen yaar,' Anurag started as Ryan cut him short.
>
> 'Just get Lost,' Ryan shouted so hard that Baku seemed to blow away just from the impact. Actually, he was shuffling backward slowly and steadily till he was almost flying in his haste to get away, the demon following suit. Anurag stood there gaping at Ryan for a while and then looked at us.[9]

Later, as he comes to realize how IIT puts a premium on blind conformism to textbooks and mugging, he is not afraid to damn the whole system as a breeding nursery of half-witted book-worms. Mark his words:

> 'Yes, but frankly, this place has let me down. This isn't exactly the cutting edge of science and technology as they describe themselves, is it?'
>
> I closed my book to join in the conversation. 'Boss, mugging is the price one pays to get the IIT tag. You mug, you pass and you get job. What letdown are you talking about?'
>
> 'That is the problem, there is this stupid system and there are stupid people like you.'

> I hate Ryan. When he is on his own trip, we all turn stupid.
>
> 'Continuous mugging, testing and assignments. Where is the time to try out new ideas? Just sit all day and get fat like Hari.'
>
> Ryan doesn't like mugging, therefore, I am stupid and fat. People like him think they are god's gifts to the world. What's worse they are.
>
> (*Five Point,* 25) (Emphasis added)

Again he dismantles the system when his teachers discourage all innovative attempts by their students. He says:

> 'I mean this is supposed to be the best college in India, the best technology institute for a country of a billion. But has IIT ever invented anything? or made any technical contribution to India?'...
>
> Ryan continued to muse. 'Over thirty years of IITs, yet, all it does is train some bright kids to work in multinationals. I mean look at MIT in the USA.'
>
> (*Five Point,* 54) (Emphasis added)

The system depresses Ryan, and he displays his *anger* in rebellious behaviour. With Hari he breaks open the staircase lock and goes to the insti-roof where they drink vodka, smoke grass and listen to pop music:

> I had gone to the insti to see the results, but that was incidental, the real reason was to chill out on the insti roof.
>
> I don't remember when we first discovered this roof, it must have been soon after we started smoking grass, which was soon after we had started vodka, which was soon after we had started listening to Pink Floyd. Floyd, vodka, grass and the insti roof; finally, we were on to what really mattered in life, the stuff that made NT life bearable, especially when you were a five-point something . . .

> If one stood up and looked down, one could see the street lights on campus roads and distant views of Kumaon and other hostels a kilometre away.
>
> Ryan laid out the vodka, the joints and his small *Walkman* in autopilot, familiar with our twice a week routine.
>
> We lay down on the concrete, still warm from the sunlight in the day. Ryan divided the pair of earphones, such that we had one earphone each, passed a joint to me, and we kept the vodka bottle in the center. Sip, puff, sip, rewind, stop and play.
>
> The lyrics washed over us and we flew up to the sky as it flew down at us.
>
> (*Five Point*, 16-11) (Emphasis added)

Ryan makes one last-ditch effort to impress his teachers. He comes up with a battery operated model of a screw-jack that may help those who were dumped with a flat tyre on the highway. Look what happens:

> Prof. Vohra walked along the class rows, looking at the familiar designs that all his students drew year after year—the simple screw-jack. His stroll ended at our desk.
>
> 'What is this?' Prof. Vohra said, twisting his head around to make sense of Ryan's unfamiliar drawing.
>
> 'Sir, this is a modified screw-jack,' Ryan said, 'It can be attached to the car's battery. . .'
>
> 'Is this an electrical engineering class?'
>
> 'No sir but the end need is the same . . .'
>
> 'Is this an internal combustion engines class?'
>
> 'Sir but . . .'
>
> 'If you don't want to be in my class or follow my course you may leave.'
>
> Prof. Vohra's face no longer looked kind. If only Ryan had kept quiet, he would have moved on.

> 'Sir, this is a new design,' Ryan said, as if it was not painfully obvious.
>
> 'Really? And who told you to do that?'
>
> Ryan did not answer, just lifted his assignment sheet. Then in one stroke, he ripped it apart in two pieces.
>
> 'There, it is useless now,' Ryan said. . . .
>
> He directly copied answers of my assignments mindlessly, and never as much as looked at the question-sheet. **Yes, our greatest designer gave up.**
>
> (*Five Point,* 118-19) (Emphasis added)

This is the dead-end for Ryan in his studies. But luckily he meets a kindred soul in Prof. Veera who encourages him to continue his research in fluid dynamics. Veera appears like *deus ex machina* to save Ryan from total alienation and disaster. Though checkmated by the system he keeps his faith in his abilities and as the story ends Prof. Veera offers him a job as a research assistant. The angry young man does not have to make any more compromises with a system that sucks. This closing scene redeems Ryan and keeps his spirits upright:

> 'Would you like to work as my RA?' Prof. Veera said. 'Research Assistant. I can get you a two-year contract. Will not pay a lot, say two thousand a month. But you live on campus, and you can continue research on Lubricants.'
>
> I saw Ryan's face. The ₹ 2000-number was writ large on his face; a third of what our jobs would pay us. Would Ryan be able to accept that?
>
> 'It is an idea,' he said eventually.
>
> 'It is a great idea. And if we find an investor who is willing to commercialize your product, who knows how successful you can be,' Prof. Veera said.
>
> Ryan looked at me. Somehow, I felt he wanted me to make a decision for him. I thought about it less than I should have, but gave me answer.
>
> 'I think you will be happy doing this, Ryan. And I am sure you will find an investor for it one day,' I said.

> 'I project the market for this product at at least ten crore. You'll get a royalty of, I don't know, say ten percent. Of course, if we find someone who invests in the factory first, Prof. *Veera* said.
>
> 'I'll do it,' Ryan smiled, 'I am your RA, sir.'
>
> 'Yes!' I said and hi-fived him.
>
> (*Five Point*, 257) (Emphasis added)

By the end the angry young man is seen smiling as he has joined his vocation with his avocation.

The second incarnation of the angry young man in Chetan Bhagat's fiction is Vroom in *One Night @ the Call Center*. Vroom is angry with the mantra of globalisation that has converted developing countries like India into sweetshops for arrogant Americans. He is self-alientated as he feels that he has sold his soul to the devil, having chosen the soft option of making good money for answering silly calls from moronic customers. How he landed at the call center is another fascinating story. Initially he worked as a journalist when he used the media to attack the political dispensation in India. In a brilliant exposition of satiric writing he worked out a lead article entitled 'Why Don't Politicians Ever Commit Suicide?' Shyam narrates the story to his girl-friend, Priyanka:

> 'Oh yeah. It was called 'Why Don't Politicians Ever Commit Suicide?"
>
> 'What? Sounds morbid.'
>
> 'Well, the article said all kinds of people—students, housewives, businessmen, employees and even film stars—commit suicide. But politicians never do. That tells you something.'
>
> 'What?' she said, still keeping her eyes down.
>
> 'Well, Vroom's point was that suicide is a horrible thing and people do it only because they are really hurt, this means they feel something. But politicians don't. So, basically, this country is run by people who don't feel anything.'

'Wow! Can't imagine that going down well with his editor.'

'You bet it didn't. However, Vroom had sneaked it in. The editor only saw it after it was printed and all hell broke loose. Vroom somehow saved his job, but his bosses moved him to page 3.'

'Our Vroom? page 3?'

'They told Vroom he was good looking, so he would fit in there. In addition, he had done a photography course. He could click the pictures himself.'

'Cover Page 3 because you are good looking? Now that sounds dumb,' she said.

'It is dumb. But Vroom took his revenge there too. He took unflattering pictures of the glitterati—faces stuffed with food, close-ups of cellulite thighs, drunk people throwing up—that sort of stuff showed up in papers the next day.'

'Oh my god,' Priyanka laughed. 'He sounds like *an* activist. I can't understand his switching to the call center for money.[10]

That ends his foray into journalism and Vroom lands at the call center. He realises he is wasting his life in such a soul-billing job but easy money has him hooked. He erupts off and on about being used as cheap labour to serve Americans. Looking at CNN news reports about the Iraq war, he says America will never bomb China and India:

'Americans *are* sick,' Vroom said, as he pointed to a US politician who had spoken out in support of the war. 'Look at him. He would nuke the whole world if he could have his way.'

'No, not the whole world. I Don't think they'd blow up China,' Priyanka said, sounding high. 'They need the cheap labour.'

'Then I guess they won't blow up Gurgaon either. They need the call centers,' Radhika said.

> 'So we are safe,' Esha said, 'that's good. Welcome to Gurgaon, the safest city on earth.'
>
> The girls started laughing. Even Military Uncle smiled.
>
> 'It's not funny girls. Our government doesn't realize this, but Americans are using us. We are sacrificing an entire generation to service their call centers,' Vroom said, convincing me that one day he could be a politician.
>
> (*ON@CC*, 199) (Emphasis added)

Vroom may join politics as he hates the guts of India's policymakers who have sucked the blood of youth. The Planning Commission does not know how to use the vast demographic power to build a new India. Vroom has these words of wisdom to offer:

> 'So like, there is so much to do. We should be building roads, power plants, airports, phone networks and metro trains in every city like madness. And if the government moves its rear-end and does that, the young people in this country will find jobs there. Hell, I would work days and nights for that, as long as I know that what I am doing is helping build something for my country, for its future. But the government doesn't believe in doing any real work, so they allow these BPOs to be opened and think they have taken care of the youth. Just as this stupid MTV thinks showing a demented chick do a dance in her underwear will make the program a youth special. Do you think they really care?'
>
> 'Who?' I said. 'The government or MTV?' I got up and signalled for the check (in bars you always ask for the check-never the bill). It was 3:50 a.m., and I had enough of Vroom's lecture. I wanted to get back to the call center soon.
>
> (*ON@CC*, 201)

Vroom's anger hits the ceiling when he learns that his devilish boss, Bakshi, has stolen his website plan to claim the credit of having designed it:

> 'It says it by fucking Subhash Bakshi,' Vroom said, tapping his finger hard on my monitor. 'Check this out. Mr. Moron, who can't tell a computer from a piano, has done this website and this manual. Like crap he has.'
>
> Vroom banged his fists on the table. In a mini-fit, he violently swept the table with his hands. All the pens fell on the floor.
>
> 'What is wrong with you?' Esha said and pulled her chair away to avoid the shower of pens. Desperately shaking the phone to get a connection, she got up and went to the conference room.
>
> 'He passed off our work as his, Shyam. Do you realize that?' he said and shook my shoulder hard.
>
> I was numb as I stared at the first page of our, or rather Bakshi's manual. This time Bakshi had bypassed himself in stealing credit. My head felt dizzy and I fought to breathe.
>
> 'This is so crap. Six months of work on this manual alone,' I said and dosed the file. 'I never thought he would stoop this low.'
>
> 'And?' Vroom said.
>
> 'And what? I don't really know what to do. I'm in shock. Plus, right now there is this fear he may downsize us...' I said.
>
> 'Downsize us?' Vroom said and stood up. 'We worked on it for six months man. And all you can say is we can't do anything as he may downsize us? This fucking loser Bakshi is turning you into a loser. Mr. Shyam, you are turning into a mousepad, people are rolling over you everyday. Priyanka tell him to say something. Go to Bakshi's office and hold his damn collar.' (*ON@CC*, 145)

To spend his pent up anger Vroom breaks his computer monitor, as he leaves with his team for a long drive across Gurgaon. They stop near a mall with Vroom raving and ranting against the neon signboards that sell worthless items like cola and pizza. He looks at a young heroine endorsing a cold drink on a hoarding and shouts:

> 'Yes, youth icon. This airhead chick is supposed to be our role model. Like she knows a fuck about life and gives a fuck about us. All she cares about is cash. She doesn't care about you or me. She just wants you to buy this black piss,' Vroom said, pointing to the cola bottle.
>
> 'Black piss?' I said and smiled. I sat down on some steps nearby.
>
> 'Do you know how much sugar there is in one of these drinks?' Vroom said.
>
> I shook my head.
>
> 'Eight spoons of sugar in every bottle—and nothing else. And yet, they convince us this is important. It isn't.'
>
> Vroom looked around and noticed a pile of bricks. He lifted one and threw it hard at the cola hoarding. Bang! It hit the actress's cheek, creating a dimple you would almost think was natural. She still kept smiling.
>
> 'Careful, for fuck's snake. Let's go back. Someone will see us and get us arrested.'
>
> 'Like I care. Nobody cares.' Vroom said and staggered towards me. I looked at his lanky outline in the street lights. 'The government doesn't care for anybody,' he continued. 'Even that *youth special* channel, they don't care either. They say youth because they want the damn *Pizza Huts* and *Cokes* and *Pepsis* of the world to come and give their ads to them.'
>
> (*ON@CC*, 254) (Emphasis added)

He is angry with himself for the soft option he has taken for the sake of a decent salary. Having broken a window, he runs and curses himself:

> 'Fuck, Let's run,' Vroom said and we sprinted towards the Qualis.

> 'I thought you liked pizza,' I said when we reached the Qualis.
>
> 'I like pizza. Damn well I do. I like jeans, mobiles and pizzas. I earn, I eat, I buy shit and I die. This is all the fuck there is to Vroom. It is all bullshit man,' Vroom said, panting and holding his stomach. He didn't look too good, but at least the run seemed to have sobered him down.
>
> (*ON@CC*, 205)

It is in his interview with God that Vroom makes an honest confession of his past errors and promises to make a fresh start in life:

> 'I want to have a life with meaning, even if it means a life without bed or daily trips to Pizza-Hut. I need to quit this call center. Sorry, but calling is not my calling,' Vroom said.
>
> (*ON@CC*, 219) (Emphasis added)

But before quitting the *call center* he has a job to do. He has to fix Bakshi for having cheated his team. First he entraps the boss with a fake email, and pushes him into a corner; his *anger* boiling over:

> 'Good. And this time, no idiot will take credit for our websites,' Vroom said and slapped Bakshi's face. Bakshi's face turned sixty degrees from the impact. He held his cheeks but remained silent, apart from a tiny dry sob. His facial expression had a combination of ninety pain and ten percent shame.
>
> 'May I?' I said.
>
> 'Be my guest,' Vroom said.
>
> Slap! I gave a slap on Bakshi's face. The face turned sixty degrees in the other direction. It was my most fun career moment. The shiny face turned hot.
>
> (*ON@CC*, 238) (Emphasis added)

The two friends, Vroom and Shyam, walk away into the sunset having avenged the wrongs they have suffered. The hope is for a morrow when they will start up their own web-design company and never be utilized as cheap labour again.

Ishaan, in *The 3 Mistakes of My Life*, is another prototype of the angry young man. He is angry for having to suffer indignities as he is from the lower middle class. The upper class boys drive swanky cars and harass innocent girls. But when such a boy begins to chase Vidya, his sister, he decides to teach the bugger a lesson:

> Beep, beep, beep. The horn of a car broke our conversation. A car zoomed outside the pol.
>
> 'What the hell! **I am going to teach this bastard a Lesson,**' Ish said, Looking out the window.
>
> 'What's up?'
>
> 'Bloody son of a rich dad. Comes and circles around our house everyday.'
>
> 'Why?' I said.
>
> 'For Vidya. He used to be in coaching classes with her. She complained about him there too,' Ish said.
>
> . . .
>
> Ish grabbed the boy's head from behind and smashed his face into the bonnet. He proceeded to strike the head light with his bat. The glass broke and the bulb hung out.
>
> 'What's your problem,' the boy said, blood spurting out of his nose.
>
> 'You tell me what's up? You like pressing horns?' Ish said.
>
> Ish grabbed his collar and gave six nonstop slaps across his face. Omi picked up the bat and smashed the windscreen. The glass broke into a million pieces. People on the street gathered around as there is nothing quite as entertaining as a street fight.
>
> The boy shivered in pain and fear, what would he tell his daddy about his broken car and face?

> Ish's dad heard the commotion and came out of the house. Ish held the boy in an elbow lock. The boy was struggling to breathe.
>
> 'Leave him,' Ish's dad said.
>
> Ish gripped him tighter.
>
> 'I said leave him,' Ish's dad shouted, 'what's going on here?'
>
> 'He has been troubling Vidya since last week,' Ish said. He kicked the boy's face with his knee and released him. The boy kneeled on the floor and sucked in air. The last kick from Ish had smeared the blood from his nose across his face.
>
> 'And what do you think you are doing?' Ish's dad asked him.
>
> 'Teaching him a lesson,' Ish said and unhooked his bat.[11]

Ish's anger is not always about personal issues. He is *angry* at India's cricket establishment for not giving breaks to worthy youngsters. Rather the team is selected on the basis of caste, creed, region and crony considerations. He believes that India has been ruined by her politicians who are corrupt, dishonest and incompetent. His anti-establishment tirades are reminiscent of the vintage *angrier*.

> 'Yeah, we played good cricket, but that's about it. We remained poor, kept fighting wars, electing the same control freaks who did nothing for the country. People's job was a government job, yuck. Nobody tooks risks or stuck their neck out. Just one corrupt banana republic marketed by the leaders as this new socialist, intellectual nation. Tanks and thinktanks, nothing else,' Ish said.
>
> 'And guess who was at the top? Which party? Secular nonsense again,' Omi joined in, opening one eye.
>
> 'Well, your right-wing types didn't exactly get their act together either,' Ish said.

> 'We will, man. We are so ready. You wait and see, elections next year and Gujarat is ours,' Omi said.
>
> 'Anyway, screw politics. My point is, that the clueless Sixties to Eighties generations is now old, and running the country. But the Nineties and the, what do they say...'
>
> 'Zeroes.'
>
> 'Yeah, whatever. The Zeroes think different. But we are being run by old fogeys who never did anything worthwhile in their primetime. The Doordarshan generation is running the Star TV generation.' Ish said
>
> I clapped. 'Wow, wisdom is free at the Team India Cricket shop.'
>
> 'Fuck off. Can't have a discussion around here. You think only you are the intellectual type. I am just a cricket coach,' Ish grumbled.
>
> (*3Mistakes,* 75) (Emphasis added)

That he is not just a shouter but can act to vindicate his words is seen in the climactic scenes of *3 Mistakes*. As Post-Godhara riots are on, Ish decides to protect Ali, a cricket prodigy who happens to be a Muslim. The Hindu mobs led by Bittoo Mama want to kill Ali but Ishaan stands firm to protect the boy. He takes on the rampaging mob with fire bombs and sheer grit. Mama tries argument, threats and brute force to subdue Ishaan, but the *angry young man* will not give way to communal forces. The scene goes on to depict the confrontation:

> Fires dotted the neighbourhood skyline. The weather didn't feel as cold as a February night should be.
>
> 'We are coming!' Mama said as his group pushed the rusted metal gate of the bank open. They came to the porch and banged on the main entrance door.
>
> 'Stop shouting Mama,' Ish said.
>
> Mama looked up to the roof.
>
> 'Where are you hiding sister-fuckers,' Mama said. The crowd hurled fire torches at us. We stood two stories high. Nothing reached us. One fire torch fell on a

> rioter and he yelped in pain. A mob may be passionate, but it can also be quite stupid. They stopped throwing torches after that.
>
> Ish kept Mama engaged.
>
> 'Mama, I was born without fear. See,' Ish said and climbed on the roof ledge.
>
> (*3 Mistakes*, 230) (Emphasis added)

Ishaan will not give up without a fight to the finish. He unlocks the door of the bank-yard where they were hiding and shouts:

> 'Fuck you Mama, come in if you have the guts,' Ish shouted and walked up to the door.
>
> 'I'll let them in anyway,' Omi said and released the bolt.
>
> 'You want to kill me? Mama, go on, kill me. Why wait,' Omi said and opened the door.
>
> 'Move aside Omi. Just tell me, where is the boy,' Mama said,
>
> 'You won't get any boy here,' Ish growled.
>
> Mama's five men held up their trishuls. We lifted our cricket weapons. One man attacked Ish. Ish blocked him with his bat.
>
> (*3 Mistakes*, 231) (Emphasis added)

The stand-off continues for a long period. Ish declares that he does not want to hurt anyone, but he will never surrender Ali to be butchered. He tells Bittoo Mama:

> 'We just want to go away,' Ish said as he held his trishul, facing Mama. Mama had a trishul too. Their eyes met. Mama's men watched the impending duel. I ran with Ali to the other end of the room. The men came running after us.
>
> 'Stop you bastards,' the man said as we reached the end of the room. One of the men went and bolted the door.
>
> (*3 Mistakes*, 246)

Ish will not give way though he is badly injured in the scuffle that follows:

> Mama and Ish were still in their face off. Each had a stern gaze. Mama rotated his trishul in his hand.
>
> One of the men turned to go back to Mama.
>
> 'I'll take care of him, you finish the boy Mama,' he said.
>
> 'Sure,' Mama said as he moved away. As he left, Mama struck his trishul at Ish's toes. Ish didn't expect it. He lost his balance and fell down next to the manager's desk.
>
> 'You are fucking weak, you know that,' Ish said....
>
> Another ball lay next to Ali's foot. Ali brushed the ball with his feet towards Ish. The ball rolled to Ish. Ish sat on the floor leaning against the manager's table. His toes whooshed out blood and he couldn't get up.
>
> (*3 Mistakes*, 247)

Ishaan's courage of conviction pays off and he manages to save Ali even at the cost of losing his friend Omi and being instrumental in the death of Bittoo Mama. This *angry young man* is a worthy example of communal harmony and dedication to one's commitment.

Krish, in *2 States,* is also *angry,* with his parents for their constant bickering; with his Punjabi community for their feelings of racial superiority; and with Indian tradition that prohibits love marriage. Ananya, his beloved, asks him about the cause of his anger regarding his family. He says:

> 'They'd have a problem with anyone I choose. And you are South Indian, which doesn't help at all. OK, it's not as bad as marrying someone from another religion. But pretty close.'
>
> 'But I also aced my college. I have an MBA from IIMA and work for HLL. And sorry to brag, but I am kind of pretty.'
>
> 'Irrelevant. You are Tamilian. I am Punjabi.'

> Ananya folded her offer letter and rearranged things in her bag.
>
> 'What? Say something?'
>
> 'Can't be part of this backward conversation,' she said. 'Please, discuss your woes with the Punjabi brethren.'
>
> She stood up to leave. I tugged her down by her hand, 'C'mon Ananya, aren't your parents going to flip out when they find out you have a Punjabi boyfriend?'[12]

Moreover, he is angry with his father for his cruel behaviour. His childhood memories are of merciless beating; even his mother was not spared. Ananya asks him if he has invited his father to the convocation at IIM. Krish does not know what to say:

> I came out of the booth. Ananya and I walked back. Which father needs a*n* invitation from his son to attend his convocation? *Screw him,* I said to myself.
>
> 'You invited him?' Ananya asked.
>
> 'Dad's not coming,' I said.
>
> 'Why?'
>
> 'We have no relationship, Ananya. Don't try and fix it ever. OK?'
>
> 'What happened though?'
>
> 'I don't want to talk about it.'
>
> 'Standard answer.'
>
> '*Yours was a standard question.*'
>
> (2 *States,* 41) (Author's emphasis)

Later he confesses to Guruji and Ananya that he carries the guilt of having hit back at his father one night. His *anger had* blinded him:

> 'So, tell me, whhat did you do? And what's with the tilak on your forehead?'
>
> 'I hit my father.'
>
> 'What?'

> 'A Long time ago. Remember, how I would always avoid talking about my father in campus?'
>
> 'Yes I never pushed after that,' she said. 'But what are you saying?'
>
> I repeated the story of that night.
>
> She looked at me, awestruck
>
> 'Oh dear, I didn't know your parents were like this.'
>
> (2 *States*, 170) (Emphasis added)

The problem of Punjabi vs. Madrasi that his mother keeps raking off and on aggravates the *anger* of Krish further. His mother wants him to marry a Punjabi girl that may fetch a huge dowry. Krish refuses point blank:

> 'I can't make out,' I said.
>
> 'You should meet her. And here, keep stirring the *bhindi* while I make the *rotis,*' She handed me the ladle.
>
> 'I don't want to meet anyone.'
>
> 'Only once.'
>
> 'What's so special about her?'
>
> 'They have six petrol pumps.'
>
> 'What?'
>
> 'Her father. He has six petrol pumps. And the best part is, they have only two daughters. So each son-in-law will get three, just imagine.'
>
> 'What?' I said as I imagined myself sitting in a gas station.
>
> 'Yes, they are very rich. Petrol pumps sell in cash. Lots of black money.'
>
> 'And what does the girl do? Is she educated?'
>
> 'She is doing something. These days you can do graduation by correspondence also.'
>
> 'Oh, so she is not even going to college?'
>
> 'College degrees you can get easily. They are quite rich.'

> 'Mom, that's not the point. I can't believe you are going to marry me to a twelfth pass...oh, forget it. Put this album away. And *are* the rotis done? I am hungry.'
>
> 'We can get an educated Punjabi girl. Do you like doctors?'
>
> 'No, I don't like any Punjabi girl.'
>
> 'Your mother is Punjabi,' my mother said in an upset tone.
>
> 'That's not the point, mom,' I said and opened the fridge to take out curd. 'I don't want any other girl. I have a girl friend.'
>
> 'You'll marry that Madrasi girl?' my mother asked, seriously shocked.
>
> (*2 States*, 58) (Emphasis added)

Krish's efforts to convince the two families are difficult enough, but the breaking point comes when Ananya's family wants to marry her off to Harish, a Tamilian NRI. Krish is very *angry* with that rival in love. He meets Harish at Ananya's house:

> 'You also went to IIMA? I have many colleagues who *are* your seniors,' Harish said.
>
> 'Really? That's nice,' I said. I wanted to shove the spiral snacks up his moustache-covered nose, but I kept a diplomatic smile.
>
> Ananya's father spoke to Harish's father in Tamil.
>
> 'Something something Citibank Chennai posted something. Something something Punjabi fellow.'
>
> Everyone nodded and felt relieved after my credentials of being a Punjabi made me a safe outsider....
>
> 'See, how much care he is taking of her already. You are so lucky, Ananya,' an aunt said as I almost tore a piece of banana leaf and ate it.
>
> I saw the bowl of sambhar in the middle. I wondered if I should pick it up and upturn it on Harish's head.

> *She can take her own idlis, idiot, why don't you go drown in Bali, I thought.*
>
> Harish thought it really funny to shift everything he was served to Ananya. He transferred parts of the upma, pongal, chutney and banana chips from his leaf to hers. *Really Harish, did nobody teach you not to stretch a bad joke too far? And all you aunts, can you please stop sniggering so as to not encourage this moron?*
>
> 'We must decide the date keeping in mind the US holiday calendar,' Shobha aunty said and felt she was moving way, way too fast.
>
> 'Easy, aunty, easy,' Ananya said.
>
> *Thanks, Ananya madam, that is so nice of you to finally impart some sense to these people.* 'You OK?' Manju offered *an* idli to me. I had spent two months with him. He could sense the turmoil in me.
>
> 'I'm good,' I said...
>
> I'm going to get you all, I will, I swore to myself as I went to wash my hands.
>
> (*2 States,* 126-27) (Author's emphasis)

The feeling of anger darkens the love-life of Krish and Ananya. When they go for a holiday to Goa to patch up the relationship between their families another squabble happens:

> 'My parents are upset,' Ananya said, 'your mother should learn to talk.'
>
> The waves splashed the shore as many tourist couples walked hand-in-hand in front of us. I bet they weren't discussing the mood swings of their future in-laws.
>
> 'Your parents should know how to behave,' I said.
>
> There we were, at one of the most romantic locations in India having our first marital discord. In an Indian love marriage, by the time everyone gets on board, one wonders if there is any love left.
>
> 'How can they behave better?' she said.

> 'I will tell you. But you must do exactly as I say,' I said.
>
> 'If it is reasonable,' said my sensible girlfriend.
>
> 'Step one, buy my mother *an* expensive gift.'
>
> 'Really?'
>
> 'Yes step two, when we go out in Goa tomorrow, always offer to pay.'
>
> 'Everywhere?'
>
> 'Yes, at restaurants, to taxis or anywhere else. And when you offer, she will say no. But insist, if needed, snatch her purse to prevent her from paying. In Punjabis, this is considered OK, even affectionate.'
>
> Ananya's jaw went slack.
>
> (*2 States,* 224) (Emphasis added)

That Krish rises above his *anger* and takes recourse to reconciliation is partly responsible for his redemption. The denouement reiterates the point that love conquers all hurdles and the world cannot stop the consummation of a true relationship.

Not only his protagonists, even Chetan Bhagat is himself something of an angry young man. If we consider his non-fiction writings, his sense of indignation and frustration with post-colonial India is quite evident. It is not the opportune moment to go in the details of Bhagat's journalism but some articles have to be mentioned as they exemplify his anger. 'The Indian Institute of Idiots' has already been referred to in Chapter-II. Some other recent lead stories done by him include angry references to Indian society and polity. In 'My Community, My Country' he writes about the divisive nature of regional politics:

> So what is the solution? How can, we check these divisive knife-wielders who are only too happy to cut up our people at the slightest provocation? What do we do about people who refuse to look at the big picture but only care about the next vote count? Here are three suggestions:

> One, any act of preference to any community which may disadvantage other Indians should be made illegal. Too many laws are never good, but anyone favouring one community is by definition harming the prospects of the others. If this is not racism, what is? And racism should be illegal, even if disguised as a welfare scheme.
>
> Second, we as Indians need to decide for once our primary loyalty—whether it is to the country or to community. If we choose country, we have a good chance of becoming a progressive nation. If we choose our state first, things won't change. Are you a change agent or are you a roadblock? Decide, and live with it.
>
> Third, Indians need to intermingle. This is not an overnight process, but migration, education outside the state, intercommunity marriages should be culturally encouraged.[13]

In another article Bhagat insists that the evils at the root of India's backwardness are servility that kills innovation, insensitive attitude that encourages corruption and divisiveness that leads to nepotism and regionalism.

He also suggests a cure for these evils:

> We need mass self-psychotherapy for the three traits listed above. When we talk of change, you and I alone can't replace a politician, or order a road to be built. However, we can change one thing—our mindset. And collectively, this alone has the power to make the biggest difference. We have to unlearn whatever is holding us back, and definitely break the cycle so we don't pass on these traits to the next generation. Our children should think creatively, have opinions and speak up in class. They should learn what is wrong is wrong, no matter how big or small. And they shouldn't hate other people on the basis of their background. Let us also resolve to start working on our own minds, right now. A change in mindset changes the way people vote, which in turn changes politicians....

> If we resolve today that we will vote on the basis of performance alone, we will encourage the voices against injustice and we will encourage the voices against injustice and we will place an honest but less wealthy person on a higher pedestal than a corrupt but rich person. By doing so, we would contribute to India's progress. If everyone who reads this newspaper did this, it would be enough to change voting patterns in the next election. And then, maybe, we will start moving towards a better India. Are you on board?[14]

In a recent write-up Chetan Bhagat has emphasised the need for setting up a new sense of values in Indian society. The basic problem for the nation, he feels, is not social or economic; it is a moral vacuum that is hurting India:

> As we enter the new decade, there will be prescriptions on how many roads, airports and power plants we need to build. Along with this infrastructure, we must spend time building our values. Leaders, opinion makers and all of us in our dinner table discussions should continue to bring up this single question. What should an average Indian live, work and strive for in his life?
>
> At present, there is no easy answer. There is also deep cynicism. But if we keep looking, and contribute to the quest for the right answer, we will find it. The answer to this fundamental question will determine our Constitution, our Laws and where we will go as a society and nation in times to come. India will grow economically in the next 10 years. But if we focus on our collective values too, it will truly be a happy new decade.[15]

Such moralising helps but it is not Chetan Bhagat at his best. He is more of a story-teller, and his anger at the ruling dispensation in New Delhi comes out brilliantly in a fable that he has written a few months back. He tells the story of a pond near a village where white swans are revered as gods. Then comes along a golden duck followed by a silent, wise duck (the PM and his backer?). The villagers worship them. Things, start to go wrong when crocodiles infest the pond and eat away the young ones. The ducks remain silent. Soon enough, the villagers realize that the ducks and crocs are hand in glove. They dig a canal and take away all the water. The unholy nexus is exposed and a new pond is created. The idea is that a corrupt government needs be thrown out and a new dispensation brought in. This is the correction Indian polity needs today. Chetan writes:

> 'Enough's enough, we have to do something ourselves,' the villagers said.
>
> Over the next few months, *they started to dig a new lake. They also made several mini-lakes at various levels of the terrace farm.* They put strong iron meshes, so the crocodiles could not enter. The villagers collected buckets of water and filled it in the new lakes. One smart villager put an underground pipe to empty out the old lake and fill the new one. *Soon, the old lake had no water. As it dried up, the crocodiles and ducks struggled to live. They begged the villagers for some water but the villagers paid no attention.*
>
> The new lakes opened, and the villagers loved them. They also realised that they made the lake, and not the other way around. Children came back to swim in the new lakes, crops had enough water and the village prospered like never before. Everyone in the old lake died. And then, the villagers lived happily ever after.[16]

This is the *angry young man* in Chetan Bhagat calling for a peaceful revolution through the ballot box. No wonder his words have mesmerized a whole generation in India. The whole congregation of youth at *Ramlila Ground* in New Delhi to support *Anna Hazare's hunger strike against corruption and crony capitalism is a tribute to the impact of his writings, both fiction and non-fiction. The anger among the youth is palpable, and a socio-political change seems to be imminent.* Consider this report in *The Times of India*:

> For Shashi Shekhar Singh, a civil engineering student from IIT Kharagpur, supporting Anna's anti-

> corruption campaign was far more important than getting his M. Tech degree at the 57th Convocation at his alma mater from chief guest, PM Manmohan Singh, on Monday. That's why this IITian didn't mind giving the convocation a miss. Even though he was in Kharagpur, he thought it was better to utilise the event as a means to spread the word and express his solidarity towards Anna's campaign. Shashi, who has allegedly been quoted as saying, 'I will not accept my degree from the Prime Minister', states he is neither against any political party nor any particular individual, and that nothing can deter him from accomplishing his goal. 'Degree ka kya hai, woh toh kal bhi mil sakti hai. Degree bahut choti cheez hai. Aur yeh andolan zyaada zaroori hai. Kisi party vishesh ke liye andolan nahin hona chahiye bas vyavastha parivartan ke liye andolan hona chahiye. This is what Mahatma Gandhi believed in and now it is the responsibility of the youth to ensure that it happens as per his dream.'
>
> Shashi's birthplace is Bihar, but he insists he should be referred to as an Indian exclusive of his regional ethnicity. Having witnessed unethical acitivities in his native state, Shashi speaks about the changes that Bihar has witnessed courtesy 'vyavastha parivartan'. 'These things used to happen earlier Lekin ab wahan pe vyavastha parivartan hai. It is corruption—a social evil which has seeped into the system and the way we seem to have grown used to it, is what needs to be eradicated. This can't be done till we work toward it together. We are not against anyone; we are in support of Anna. If Bihar can improve, I'm sure India can also become a better placed.'[17]

This is voice of youth that Chetan Bhagat represents—a voice of constructive anger for the common good.

Notes

1. Eagleton M. and Pierre D: *Attitudes to Class in the English Novel* (London, Thames and Hudson, 1979) p. 141.

2. John Wain: *Hurry on Down* (Harmondsworth, Penguin Boobs, 1960) p. 64 (All subsequent citations are from this edition and the page no's have been given in parenthesis)
3. James Gindin: *Post-War British Fiction*: (Berkley, Univ. of California Press, 1962) p. 91.
4. G.S. Fraser: *The Modern Writer and His World.* (Harmondsworth, Penguin Boobs, 1964) p. 175.
5. Malcolm Bradbury: *The Modern British Novel* (Harmondsworth, Penguin books, 1994) p. 320.
6. Kigsley Amis: *Lucky Jim*: (Harmondsworth, Penguin, 1976) p. 8. (All subsequent citations are from this edition and the page no's have been given in parenthesis)
7. John Braine: *Room at the Top*: (Harmondsworth, Penguin Books, 1975) p.8. (All subsequent citations are from this edition and the page no's have been given in parenthesis)
8. Malcolm Bradbury: *The Modern British Novel*, p. 324.
9. Chetan Bhagat: *Five Point Someone* p. 6 (Emphasis added)
10. Chetan Bhagat: *One Night at the Call Center* p. 49 (Emphasis added)
11. Chetan Bhagat: *The 3 Mistakes of My Life,* pp. 3-5 (Emphasis added)
12. Chetan Bhagat: *2 States* p. 40 (Emphasis added)
13. Chetan Bhagat: 'My Community, My Country', *The Times of India,* Delhi, January 30, 2010. p. 14.
14. Chetan Bhagat: 'The Great Indian Psychotherapy' *Sunday Times of India* Delhi, September 26, 2010 p. 18.
15. Chetan Bhagat: 'Adding Values to Life' *The Times of India,* Delhi, January 1, 2011, p. 12.
16. Chetan Bhagat: 'Of Ducks and Crocodiles' *The Times of India*, Feb., 26, 2011 p. 16. (Emphasis added)
17. Divya Pal: 'Degree Chhoti Cheez Hai' *The Times of India,* Delhi, August 14, 2011, p. 2.

Conclusion

6

Chetan Bhagat is the one English novelist of contemporary India who has changed the rules of the game. He is not looking for literary awards or laurels in academic corridors; he is rather looking to enthrall his young audience with a curious blend of heady romance, gentle irony, bitter satire and occasional shots of pathos. His dark comedies have caught the pulse of the urban Indian youth who have had enough of status quo and want something somewhere to change. His best-sellers are entertaining, but they are not Chicklet-fiction by any stretch of imagination. By his own admission his works are ninety percent entertainment and ten percent moralising. But that ten percent is crucial in raising his novels as calls for socio-political activism; to move the youth from blind conformism to an awakened rebellion. If the sleeping giant that India is, needs a kick in the pants to wake up, his protagonists like Ryan, Vroom and Ishaan are more than willing to oblige. Whatever the haughty highbrow critics may say, Chetan Bhagat has gate-crashed into their musty chambers, and it is impossible to deny him the status of being India's leading English novelist today. A recent post at the Internet goes:

> Salman Rushdie, Anita Desai, Amitav Ghosh. If you have to describe Indian Literature written in English, words like highbrow and worthy come to mind. But while the country's serious writers—most recently Aravind Adiga—continue to attract international acclaim, domestically they are being overshadowed by a new breed of authors led by Chetan Bhagat.

> The books produced by this generation are not about partition, or the Emergency, or three-generational family sagas written in oxford English, says New Delhi literary agent Renuka Chatterjee.[1]

In popular fiction the topics are populist and contemporary (college, finding a job, looking for love) and English is as unpretentious as in a call center cubicle. At the same time, these novels still do what novels have always done: serve as guides in a confusing world.

> Suddenly, everything has changed so much, says novelist and publisher Namita Gokhale. So people use these books to try to find where—they're located in all this.[2]

And that has made the new fiction a runaway success. Helped additionally by low prices and new distribution channels (the books are sold on street corners and in department-store chains like Big Bazaar, not just in conventional books stores), first-time authors are moving into the best-seller category.

At the top of the new generation is Chetan Bhagat, whom fellow author Anirban Bose calls the Tenzing Norgay and Edmund Hillary of Indian mass-market publishing[3] Bhagat's three books, the first of which was published in 2004, have sold more than a million copies. Chetan Bhagat's success has demonstrated that there is a huge market for Indian fiction, with everyday Indian characters acting out everyday Indian stories. Publishers have taken note that homegrown talent is finding a voice, and that publishing new authors could actually be profitable.

With his chubby face and rumpled clothes, Bhagat neither looks nor aspires to a be an academic big-wig. He looks much more like an overworked investment banker that he was before the success of his first book, *Five Point Someone,* a campus novel following three best friends at the Indian Institute of Technology (IIT) in New Delhi, took him by surprise:

> I didn't have the baggage of other Indian authors, ... I just wanted to write a fun book.[4]

And so he did—the characters get drunk, fall in love and steal exam papers—but *Five Point Someone* also taps into the pressures facing students at India's elite educational institutions. One character's brilliant research proposal gets shelved because he's considered an underachiever, with a five-point-something grade average. Another nearly breaks down under the pressure from his mother to find a job that will pay for his father's medical bills and sister's dowry. Bhagat could have written a post-graduation sequel but instead he tried to get closer to the average young Indian by setting his second book, *One Night @ the Call Center,* in a workplace familiar to many of them. In his next novel, released in 2008, he ventured out to the provinces, following three cricket-mad friends who start a business in the western Indian city of Ahmedabad. Entitled *The 3 Mistakes of My Life,* the book has already sold 500,000 copies, thanks to a text that is accessible to readers whose first language isn't English. The author cheekily says:

> These kids may have only studied English as a subject in school, and they might not be able to read any other novel in English, . . . but they can read a Chetan Bhagat novel.[5]

You may love him or hate him, but Chetan Bhagat's big contribution to Indian publishing has been to bring out of the woodwork a whole segment of readers that publishers had traditionally believed never existed. His readers are college and high school students, the under-25s, whom the high-brow critics liked to believe would rather buy a pizza or go disco-dancing than spend money on a book. But they will buy books relevant to their own lives. Amitabha Bagchi, author of another IIT novel, *Above Average*, says :

> Young Indians want to read about themselves not entirely as an act of narcissism but also as part of a process of adapting to, and learning to live in, a social milieu that is evolving faster than most people can comprehend.[6]

The uncompromising modernity of Chetan Bhagat is also a remarkable feature. Reading his novels one gets a sense of defiance in his choosing to write about the present—an insistence that the stories of how Indians live now are just as worthy of being told as the more self-consciously literary sagas set in some supposedly more romantic past. Indian best-seller fiction might be banished to second-class status by critics, says Bhagat, but it's not that to the people who read it. For them, it tells the stories of their own lives, and looks ahead of India's thrilling if uncertain future. See what Chetan Bhagat has done to the Indian youth. Whether his stories inspired the youth in right way or not but many young professionals across the country have turned English authors by night. Some of them are even the best-sellers! Anyhow it's a good scenario to see young people not just reading but also writing. Indians have got some variety, a lot of new and relevant fiction to read.

Chetan's four books till date, *Five Point Someone, One Night at the Call Center, The 3 Mistakes of My Life, 2 States,* are all based on the lives of young Indians. These books have reminded today's youth about their college life, love stories and inspired them to social activism. He has also inspired other young writers. Many think that one has to be a scholar or at least a student of literature and have lot of life experience to write books. But now any keen observer of life can write books. The success of Chetan Bhagat's books has inspired the publishers to believe in today's youth and their simple stories.

In his very first novel, Five Point Someone, Chetan Bhagat worked out his formula of success. He made up his dark comedy with a concoction of humour, anger, love, frustration and youthful exuberance. The narrator, Hari, presents a collage of emotions and events in the elitist world of India's most prestigious engineering institute. The comedic plot is simple. Hari, Ryan and Alok spend four years in Kumaon hostel at the IIT Delhi. Alok is short, and portly with thick glasses. He comes from a poor family. His mother is a teacher and the only breadwinner for the family as his father is paralyzed and bed-ridden. He is desperate to graduate, find a good job to maintain his family and also financially help his elder sister get married. Ryan is handsome, and well off financially. He has spent most of his life in a boarding school and hates his parents. He is the most creative of the three and is more fun-loving. He is soon fed up with strict IIT's academic regimen of lectures, tutorials, quizzes, vivas and tests that leave little time for fun. A C2D (Cooperate to dominate) plan is hatched, whereby they take turns to attend classes and share notes, etc. Ryan gets a Kinetic Honda which they use for sightseeing, going to movies, restaurants, and visits to Alok's home. They also frequent a roadside food joint for butter-paranthas, lemonade and cigarettes. But the most enjoyable and relaxing place for them is the roof of the eight-storey Institute building. Here they drink vodka; smoke joints and listen to Pink Floyd music. Blossoming love between Hari and Neha is also amusing and heartwarming. Cute-looking, fashion-design student Neha, daughter of the strict IIT Professor Cherian, while driving in her car, knocks down Hari who is out jogging. And they become friends. They call each other once-a-month, meet in ice-cream parlours and share ice-creamy kisses! The scene where Hari, with Ryan and Alok's help climbs the roof of Neha's home at midnight and then sneaks into her bedroom to wish her a happy birthday and offer her flowers (that too plucked from her garden!) is hilarious.

How hard they try, and despite trying various stratagems, they just cannot improve their grades. Hari always gets tongue-tied in vivas (even after downing vodka!). In the final year, Ryan thinks of Operation Pendulum-a-Mission impossible type plan-to steal the Test Paper from Prof. Cherian's office. Hari manages to borrow the bunch of keys from Neha, and gets a duplicate of the key to Cherian's office. They get caught red-handed and are punished by the Disco (Disciplinary Committee) by suspension for one semester. However, Prof. Veera, appears like a *deus ex machinato* save their careers and the book ends on an optimistic note.

His second novel, *One Night @ the Call Center,* goes down one notch on the social ladder and looks at the lives and ambitions of those who fail to qualify for professional studies. He has placed the youth factor and interesting elements in call center superbly and won the hearts of millions of his book readers. He got good help from his cousins working in call centres and personally visited some call centres to understand the environment. He had enough substance like layoffs, night shifts, pay package, bossism, and romantic love with the call center backdrop. He has carved wonderful characters like a troubled love pair with the conflict of comparatively less package for the guy, a girl striving hard to click in modelling, a married lady sacrificing everything for her family yet getting ditched, a gen-x guy who is an innovator all under a Bad Boss, struggling to save their jobs.

The main highlight of the book is not the content but the narration mode he has chosen. He starts with a fairy tale of travelling in a train and a girl sitting beside narrating him the story on the condition that he would pen it as his second book. This prologue is so mesmerizing that one would vote full marks just by reading this.

However, the climax is still more enthralling when the group of friends are trapped over a precipice and then get a phone-call from God. God advises them to heed the call of conscience and rebuild their lives on honest foundations. That night changes their lives forever and for the better.

The 3 Mistakes of My Life is the third novel written by Chetan Bhagat. The book was published in May 2008 and had an initial print-run of 420,000. The novel follows the story of three friends and is based in the city of Ahmedabad during the *Post-Godhara* turbulence. Govind Patel is a young Gujarati boy—who has scored centum in Mathematics and aspires to be a great business man. He sets up a sports goods shop with his friend and partner Ish and Omi. Ish is a cricket fanatic, a district level player turned coach. Omi is from a priest family but not interested in becoming a priest. Track-One is how Govind aspires big, manages to grow his business and goes through its ups and downs. The Gujarat earthquake ruining his over 1 lakh investment for a shop in a newly built mall is termed mistake number 1.

Govind also gives maths tuitions to earn money and he is asked to give tuition to Ish's sister. Vidya needs some help understanding maths and Govind becomes her private tutor. Track Two is how their private tuition progresses to friendship, love and more, before finally getting caught by Ish resulting in collapse of their friendship and Govind branded as a traitor. Govind violating an unwritten protocol and falling in love with his best friend's sister is termed mistake number 2.

Ish spots a young Muslim boy named Ali who due to superfast reflex is able to make mental calculations at unbelievable speeds using which he can hit sixes of every ball. The third track of the story line is as to how they struggle to make this gifted boy a superstar by coaching him, taking him to Australia and protecting him during the communal riots. A split second delay by Govind in making a specific move which could have saved Ali from a hit is termed mistake number 3.

Do these events really qualify as mistakes? All of us lose money due to bad decisions and unexpected circumstances. Most of us fall in love (one sided at least) and at some point in our life we do think and act selfish. Nobody feels anything unique about these mistakes. But Chetan uses these ideas to narrate a racy story. He gives real near life description of why many students hate maths, a kind of inside view of election politics and Gujarat riots, the challenges and differences people face while chasing big dreams and more, all in all giving the reader his money's worth. The story begins with Govind writing an email to Chetan after consuming sleep pills as a suicide attempt due to his 3 mistakes. Chetan finds and meets this guy and story begins with a flashback. Excluding the death of several people during the communal riots (including Omi, his cousin and Mama) the story otherwise has an happy ending.

The central metaphor used by Bhagat is the game of cricket. Life, like cricket, affords a second innings and one should not be despressed by initial failure. Secondly cricket is a unifying force in India's divisive polity. The game encourages a Pan-Indian sensibility.

Pan-Indian identity is also the theme of Bhagat's latest work, *2 States*. It is partially based on the author's own experiences of marriage and love. His new book, he says:

> is a social comment on homogeneity, told entertainingly. Romance never goes out of fashion.

> Everyone wants that one person who'd love them forever.[8]

This book, an autobiographical tale about an inter-caste love marriage, was launched by Minister of State for External Affairs, Shashi Tharoor. It takes off on his own marriage to a Tamil Brahmin. *2 States* is the story of his marriage and he has dedicated the book to his in-laws. He comments:

> I think this is the first time any Indian writer has dedicated a book to his in-laws, . . . The book is funny and completely different from *Five Point Someone, One Night @ the Call Center* and *The 3 Mistakes of My Life,* I did not want to write about friends any more.[9]

2 States, is about Krish and Ananya, who are from two different States of India. They are deeply in love and want to get married. But their parents do not agree. To convert the love story into a wedding, the couple have a tough fight ahead of them. Chetan Bhagat has these words to offer:

> Indian love marriages are not easy. It's not just the boy and the girl who fall in love. Everyone, both their clans, have to fall in love. In the end, the boy and the girl start questioning whether there's anything more left to it and even fight. But it's important, at least for me, what parents think of your marriage, . . .
>
> My wife read the book and loved the female lead, who is modern, liberated and educated. India is opening up and parents are learning to accept love marriages despite prejudices about caste, or region.[10]

Chetan's books are normally a bind of an interview, a talk, a chat between one of the characters and the reader. It is not a third person account, it is not Chetan who is speaking, it is a character in the story who tells the story from his perspective. This is his favourite narrative mode—the central or peripheral point of view. The first person account story telling is more realistic. The language used in his books, is simple, no flowery words, no over the head exaggeration. It's simple. The reader does not need to go grab his dictionary after every four lines.

His books are a mix of fiction and reality, presented in a language that is simple and understandable. The way he describes the intimate relations between the male and female leads, how they do the deed, is another issue which may upset some people. But the fact is that Chetan has outgrown Mills and Boon. The Bhagat dilemma is in many ways similar to the notion that Hip-Hop/Rap is not real music. Singers who have rehearsed for years and years but are nowhere in terms of record sales and fan following complain about decline in standards. They often say that popular music is not real music, something Chetan Bhagat has heard one time too many. Hip-hop/Rap sells more for a reason, it appeals to the people and people can relate to it. Eminem's songs are lyrics at best. He might not be going to the highest octet, but his songs have meaning, every word has a reason, therefore it sells. People who are not regular readers enjoy his books, because they are simple in language, true to daily life. Chetan's books have a reason, a message that is put in simple ways and not in the most boring ways like A Monk Who Sold His Ferrari. People reading his books need to look beyond the language and words used, they need to look at the psychology of the characters, the behavourial tendencies of the characters, the response to situations by the characters and at the bigger message that the book is trying to convey.

Chetan Bhagat's novels are best-sellers that display the rebellious mood of the new generation in the Indian Metros. These are dark comedies with a large emotional quotient, but Chetan holds on desperately to one idea—there are no losers in life. He tells the readers to live happily even when circumstances may not be favourable. Good days follow on bad, and there always is a dawn after midnight. What Chetan Bhagat is trying to communicate can best be defined with reference to an article by Sudhamati Regunathan, who writes:

> The premium is on winning, whatever you do, you have to win, whether it is learning to sing, dance or just play. We live in fear of losing. We fear it so much that often. We hear this being said to someone. 'You 're such a loser!'

> So what happens when you lose? Besides the fact that winning and losing are relative terms, it is really not so bad to lose once in a while. Sometimes, by losing, you could gain more, particularly when you live in a society where you are in constant touch with other people and are exposed to various situations. It is the one who loses, so to say, who actually keeps rolling. This is not to glorify losing, but to turn the focus to a balanced development rather than glorify the obsession to win always.
>
> To keep activity going, to maintain harmony and balance, we have to experience both, winning and losing. This way, the cosmic play ensures that the cycle goes on. At a mundane level, the see-saw effect creates opportunities for all. When success and failure are experiences in turn, it helps us cultivate several perspectives, to lose gracefully as well as embrace achievements with deep humility . . .
>
> This is the secret of happy togetherness. In the androgynous form, too, there was togetherness, but of a static kind. There seemed no purpose, no outcome. When they split to become two distinct entities, they could let their creations flourish. And yet they stayed together enjoying the game they played. That is togetherness; where otherness enhances the togetherness.[11]

This is exactly what Chetan Bhagat wants to convey in his best-selling black comedies of contemporary India. It will be opportune to conclude with a quote from Chetan Bhagat about what he feels his role is as a novelist. A Net post say:

> I met lots of readers and found out that while people read my books for fun, to many the books mean a lot. People have said they have become better people after reading my books and they see me as a role model. I don't think I deserve that much love, but do feel my life belongs to my readers now. To make them happy—whether for pure entertainment or being a positive influence in their life—is my key life goal.[12]

Notes

1. Net Entry : www.chetanbhagat.com/blog
2. Net entry : www.chetanbhagat.com/fancafe/blog/
3. Net entry : www.chetanbhagat.com/books/
4. Net Entry : www.chetanbhagat.com
5. Net entry : en.wikipedia.org/wiki/Chetan_Bhagat
6. Net Entry : www.chetanbhagat.com/blog
7. Net entry : www.chetanbhagat.com/about/
8. Net Entry : www.chetanbhagat.com/blog
9. Net entry : www.chetanbhagat.com/about/
10. Net Entry : www.chetanbhagat.com/blog
11. Sudhamati Regunathan: 'Are you A Loser? Good For You'. New Delhi: *The Times of India,* February 8, 2010, p. 14.
12. Net Entry : www.chetanbhagat.com/blog

Bibliography

Primary Sources

Chetan Bhagat: *Five Point Someone—What Not to Do at IIT* (Delhi, Rupa & Co., 2004)

——: *One Night @ the Call Center* (Delhi, Rupa & Co., 2005)

——: *The 3 Mistakes of My life* (Delhi, Rupa & Co., 2008).

——: *2 States* (Delhi, Rupa & Co., 2009)

Secondary Sources

A.C. Bhaktivedanta: *Bhagvadgita-As It Is* (Mumbai, Bhaktivedanta Book Trust, 2010)

Arnold Kettle: *An Introduction to English Novel* (Vol. II) (Delhi, Universal, 1990)

Amis, K.: *Lucky Jim* (Harmondsworth, Penguin, 1980).

——: *That Uncertain Feeling* (Harmondsworth, Penguin, 1959).

——: *I Like It Here* (Harmondsworth, Penguin, 1960).

Allsop, K.: *The Angry Decade* (London, MacMillan, 1966)

Allen, *Walter: Tradition and Dream: The English and American Novel from the Twenties to Our Times.* (London: J. M. Dent and Sons Ltd., 1964).

Alter, Robert: *Partial Magic: The Novel as a Self-Conscious Genre* (Berkeley: University of California Press, 1975).

Anderson, Michael: *Anger and Detachment: A Study of Arden, Osborne and Pinter.* (London: Putnam Publishing, 1976.)

Armstrong, William A: *Experimental Drama.* (London: G. Bell and Sons, 1963.)

Braine, *J.: Room at the Top* (Harmondsworth, Penguin, 1957).

——: *Life at the Top* (Harmondsworth, Penguin, 1962).

Bradbury, M.: *The Modern British Novel* (Harmondsworth, Penguin, 1993).

Bainham, Martin: *Osborne*, (Edinburgh, Oliver and Boyd, 1969.)

Brown, John Russell. (Ed.): *Modern British Dramatists.* (Englewood Cliffs, N.J.: Prentice Hall, 1968.)

Brown, John Russell: *Theatre Language: A Study of Arden, Osborne, Pinter and Wesker.* (New York: Taplinger, 1972.)

Carter, Alan: *John Osborne,* (Edinburgh: Oliver and Boyd, 1973.)

Camus, Albert: *The Collected Fiction of Albert Camus* — (London, Hamish Hamilton, 1965)

Eagleton M. And Pierre D.: *Attitudes to Class in the English Novel* (London, Thames and Hudson, 1979)

Ferrar, Harold: *John Osborne.* (New York: Columbia University Press, 1973.)

Fraser, G.S.: *The Modern Writer and His World.* (England: Penguin Books Ltd., 1964).

Gindin, James: *Postwar British Fiction, New Accents and Attitudes.* (Berkley and Los Angles, University of California, 1963).

Ginsberg, A.: *Howl and Other Poems* (New York, Viking, 1956)

Goscoigne, Bamber: *Twentieth Century Drama.* (London: Hutchinson University Library, 1962.)

Hawkes, Terence (Ed.): *New Accents.* (London and New York, Methuen, 1980).

Hewison, R. *In Anger: Culture in the Cold War* (London, Macmillan, 1981)

Hinchliffe, Arnold P.: *John Osborne.* (Boston: Twayne Publishers, 1984.)

Issacs, J.: *The Assessment of Twentieth Century Literature.* (London : Secker and Warburg, 1951).

James Mersmann: 'Allen Ginsberg' in *American Writes* (ed.) A.W. Litz, Supp. II Vol. I (New York, Scribner's, 1981)

John Femes: 'Q.D. Leavis Criticism: The Human Core' *Modern Age,* Spring 2003.

Karl, F.R.: *A Reader's Guide to the Contemporary English Novel* (London: Thames and Hudson, 1972).

Kerr, Walter: *The Theatre in Spite of Itself.* (New York: Simon and Schuster, 1963.)

Kerouac, J.: *On the Road* (New York, Viking, 1957).

Kitchen, Lawrence : *Mid-century Theatre.* (London: Faber and Faber, 1960.)

Lodge, David: *The Novelist at the Crossroads* (London: Routledge and Kegan Paul, 1971).

Lodge, D.: *The Modes of Modern Writing* (London: Routledge and Kegan Paul, 1977).

Marwick, Arthur: *British Society Since 1945* (Harmondsworth, Penguin, 1972)

Maschler, Tom (Ed.): *Declaration.* (New York: E.P. Dutton and Co., 1958.)

McCarthy, Mary: *A New Word: Sights and Spectacles.* (London: William Heinemann, 1959.)

Merton, Robert K.: *The American Soldier* (Philadelphia : Philadelphia University Press, 1964).

Miliband, Ralph: *Marxism and Politics* (London: Oxford University Press, 1977).

Morris, Robert K. (Ed): *Old Lines, New Forces: Essays on the Contemporary British Novel,* 1960-1970. (London: Associated University Presses Inc. 1976).

Newbolt, Henry: *The Poems of Matthew Arnold* (London: Thomas Nelson and Sons, 1970).

O'Connor, W. J. (Ed.): *Forms of Modern Fiction* (Bloomington: Midland Books, Indian University Press, 1959).

Osborne, J.: *Look Back in Anger* (New Delhi, Oxford University Press, Rpt. 1992).

——: *Luther* (London, Faber, 1967)

——: *Time Present* (London, Faber, 1967)

Osborne, J.: *A Better Class of Person: An Autobiography.* (London: Oxford University Press, 1981).

——: *Almost A Gentleman* (London: Oxford University Press, 1991).

Parkinson, T.F. (Ed.): *A Case Book on the Beats* (New York, University Press, 1961)

Paul Tillich: *The Courage to Be* (New Haven, Yale University Press, 1952).

Pollard, Arthur (Ed.): *Webster's New World Companion to English and American Literature* (London: Compton Russell, 1973).

Q.D. Leavis: *Collected Essays* (Vol. I) (London, Chatto and Windus, 1970).

Redford, R.: *The Progress of Romance: The Politics of Popular Fiction.* (New York, Scribner's, 1973).

Rippier, Joseph S.: *Some Postwar British Novelists* (Frankfurt: Verlag Mortiz Diesterweg, 1965).

Salwak, Dale: *John Wain* (Boston: Twayne Publishers, 1981).

Schorer, M. (Ed.): *Modern British Fiction - Essays in Criticism* (New York: Oxford University Press, 1961).

Scott-James, R.A.: *Fifty Years of English Literature*, 1900-1950 (London: Longmans, 1971).

Smith, David: *Socialist Propaganda in The Twentieth Century British Novel* (London: Macmillan, 1978)

Sinfield, A.: *Literature, Politics and Culture in Postwar Britain.* (London, Faber, 1989).

Sked, Alan and Cook, Chris: *Postwar Britain: A Political History* (London, John Murray, 1979)

Stevenson, R.: *The British Novel Since: The Thirties.* (London: Oxford University Press, 1986).

Taylor, John Russell: *Anger and After.* (London, MacMillan, 1963.)

Taylor, John Russell (Ed.): *John Osborne: Look Back in Anger*: A *Casebook*. (London: Macmillan, 1968.)

Trussler, Simon: *The Plays of John Osborne: An Assessment*, (London: Victor Gollancz, 1969.)

Tynan, Kenneth: *Curtains*. (London, Longman, 1961.)

Tytell, John: *Naked Angels: The Lives and Literature of the Beat Generation* (New York, Harper, 1976)

Vansittart, P.: *In the Fifties*: (London, Faber and Faber, 1995)

Vikram Seth: *A Suitable Boy* (Delhi, Penguin Books, 1993)

Vinson, James and Kirkpatrick (Eds.): *Contemporary Novelists* (London: St. James Press, 1976).

Watt, Ian: *The Rise of the Novel* (London: Oxford University Press, 1972).

Wellwarth, George E.: *Theatre of Protest and Paradox: Development in the Avant-Garde Drama*. (New York: New York University Press, 1964.)

Williams, Raymond: *Drama from Ibsen to Brecht: A Critical Account and Revaluation*. (Harmondsworth, Middlesex: Penguin, 1983.)

West, Paul: *The Modern Novel* (2 vols.) (New York: Hillary House, 1965).

Williams, Linda R.: *The Twentieth Century* (London, Bloomsbury, 1994).

Wain, J.: *Hurry on Down* (Harmondsworth, Penguin, 1976).

——: *Living in the Present* (Harmondsworth, Penguin, 1955)

——: *The Contenders* (Harmondsworth, Penguin, 1958)

Journals

John Fernes: 'Q.D. Leavis Criticism : The Human Core' *Modern Age,* Spring 2003

'Five Points, paranthas, and some friends' *The Hindu,* Tuesday, May 25, 2004

Chetan Bhagat: 'The Indian Institute of Idiots' *The Times of India,* Delhi; December, 2009.

Swami: Sukhbodhananda: 'Of Success And Failure', New Delhi, *The Times of India,* April 6,2011.

Janina Gomes: 'Wrestling with God' Delhi, *The Times of India,* July 27, 2010

Chetan Bhagat: 'My Community, My Country', *The Times of India,* Delhi, January 30, 2010

Chetan Bhagat: 'The Great Indian Psychotherapy' *Sunday Times of India*, Delhi, September 26,2010

Chetan Bhagat: 'Adding Values to Life' *The Times of India,* Delhi, January 1, 2011

Chetan Bhagat : 'Of Ducks and Crocodiles' *The Times of India,* Feb., 26,2011

Divya Pal: 'Degree Chhoti Cheez Hai' *The Times of India,* Delhi, August 14, 2011

Sudhamati Regunathan: 'Are you A Loser? Good For You'. New Delhi: *The Times of India*, February 8, 2010

Websites

http://timesofindia.indiatimes.com/city/bangalore/22. 11.2009

Net entry: www.chetanbhagat.com/blog.

Net entry: en.wikipedia.org/wiki/Chetan_Bhagat

Net entry: www.chetanbhagat.com/about/